TAXES, ASSETS & HEIRS

TAXES, ASSETS & HEIRS

PERSONAL WEALTH MANAGEMENT
FOR BUSINESS OWNERS

BILL HRAPMANN, CFP® CRPC®
CHAD HRAPMANN, MBA

DISCLAIMER

Securities and advisory services offered through LPL Financial, a registered investment advisor (Member FINRA/SIPC). LPL Financial and Bill Hrapmann Wealth Advisor, Inc. are separate entities.

The opinions voiced in this material are for general information only and are not intended to provide specific advice or recommendations for any individual.

The information provided is not intended to be a substitute for individualized legal or tax advice. Please consult your legal or tax advisor regarding your specific situation.

All investing involves risk including loss of principal. No strategy ensures success or protects against loss.

LIONCREST PUBLISHING

TAXES, ASSETS & HEIRS
Personal Wealth Management for Business Owners

ISBN HARDCOVER: 978-1-5445-3072-7
PAPERBACK: 978-1-5445-3071-0
EBOOK: 978-1-5445-3073-4

CONTENTS

INTRODUCTION

Your achievement mindset earned you the success you have today, and it can guide you toward even more future successes when utilizing the concepts and strategies in this book. *Taxes, Assets, and Heirs* will showcase multiple strategies in tax planning, asset protection, and educating heirs. This book will inform you of available options and remind you that, as a business owner, you have the resources to work with professionals to implement these strategies.

Only 30% of people maintain wealth through the third generation.[1] While you may not have known this exact statistic, you are aware that not every business garners the same level of success once it is bequeathed to an heir. You have spent a lifetime sacrificing and building wealth. You deserve an optimum plan to help you pursue your objectives for both you and your family. As you and your adult children grow older, you may begin to wonder, *Will I be part of the 70% who fail or among those who make it?*

Set your fears aside for a moment and imagine it is two or three years from today: You have read this book and reviewed the options available and are feeling confident about the financial decisions you have made. You are working toward reducing your taxes; you are accumulating the financial assets to live the life you have dreamed of; you are setting up your estate to be passed on to your heirs efficiently and on your terms. In summary, your finances align with

---

1 Roy Williams and Vic Preisser, *Preparing Your Heirs: Five Steps to a Successful Transition of a Family* (Oregon: Robert Reed Publishers, 2010).

both your business and personal objectives like never before. You deserve this.

Before diving into specific strategies, it is important to understand the structure of this book, so you can better use it to your advantage. **Chapter 1** focuses on wealth management for business owners, the benefits of utilizing an Optimal Financial Team, and financial concepts, such as separating business and personal assets. This chapter helps you create clear objectives and maximize your financial success. In **Chapters 2–5**, you will read about the namesakes of this book (Chapter 2 on income *taxes*, Chapter 3 on estate *taxes*, Chapter 4 on *asset* protection and preservation, and Chapter 5 on educating your *heirs*). In **Chapter 6**, you will learn about all of the relevant professionals who can help you achieve your financial objectives.

TAXES

Your tax professional may not know all of your objectives, which may lead to missed opportunities in tax savings. You must communicate openly and consistently with your tax professional, CPA, and wealth advisor to ensure they all understand your objectives, so they can utilize additional savings strategies that are right for you. Getting aligned with your objectives may help your professionals lower your taxes.

In **Chapters 2 and 3**, you will read about both the more common and advanced income tax and estate tax strategies, ranging from captive insurance policies and donor-advised funds to qualified retirement plans and gifting company shares. Discuss these ideas with your tax professional to see which methods will work for your purposes.

ASSETS

Your home, cars, warehouse, company truck—it does not matter what, why, or how you have accumulated your assets. What matters most is that your assets are protected and that you are protected from your assets (if one of your company vehicles injures a pedestrian, for example).

Whether the shortfalls are in mixing personal and business assets or in insurance coverage, you will see how important it is to have an open table with your professionals when reviewing asset protection. There are certain questions you may not know to ask, and you should not; you are not an insurance or financial expert. The guidance in these chapters will inform you on what to ask and who to collaborate with to ensure your assets do not become someone else's.

In **Chapter 4**, we will discuss options which strive to protect both your business and personal assets. Using the asset protection strategies in this chapter, such as establishing different trusts and procuring specialty insurances, you can manage the longevity of your assets now and in the generations to come.

HEIRS

Earning and maintaining wealth is no easy feat. Planning how your heirs will access and sustain that wealth is even more challenging.

Even if your heirs do not plan to run your business after you step down or pass away, make no mistake: it is still important to educate them on your financial strategies. If your heir is not privy to elements such as phantom income, they could unknowingly receive large tax bills well over six figures. They may have to borrow to pay the taxes or close the business altogether. Ensure that your legacy survives long after you do.

In **Chapter 5**, you will learn sound strategies to prepare and protect your heirs. Many of these strategies will be familiar to you after reading Chapters 2 through 4, but Chapter 5 will examine them in a new light.

As a business owner, you have put a lot of work and sacrifice into making your business successful. Your CPA, wealth advisor, tax attorney, and other professionals can plan your finances, detail your objectives, and ensure that you plan well for your future. You and your family deserve this. Tax laws are changing, and you may ask yourself, with interest rates so low and inflation rising, if your assets will remain lucrative enough to carry through to the next generations with the same quality of life. In **Chapter 6**, you will become familiar with the financial professionals who can help you achieve your financial objectives and establish your Optimal Financial Team.

The information in this book comes from over forty years of advising business owners and working with their CPAs, tax attorneys, investment bankers, business valuation specialists, and other experts, as needed.

Bill Hrapmann: Wealth Advisor—and Writer

For most of this book, you will read simple definitions for strategies your financial professionals can employ to better maintain and manage your wealth. We believe it is important to separate our personal experiences from this content because it is relevant whether we are the ones explaining them or not. We do believe it is also important for you to know, however, that the people educating you about financial strategies have the credentials to teach in this subject matter. In most chapters, we will share an anecdote about a client experience or myself, starting now:

My interest in finances developed when I was in high school. I was cutting a neighbor's grass once, and he had a Standard and Poor's Stock Guidebook. He brought it out to show me, and he said, "Do you know what dividends are? Every quarter, this company pays me a certain amount in dividends." That was the first time I heard that word. Once my interest was piqued, I made my first investment into a high-yielding "money market" while still in high school (money markets were new at the time). In college, I moved on to my first growth mutual fund investment.

I earned a business degree at Tulane University and continued my education at the University of New Orleans, receiving an MBA degree. Enrolling in the College for Financial Planning, I earned the Certified Financial Planner™ (CFP®) certification and took additional courses in estate planning. Later in my career, I was drawn to the area of retirement planning and ensuring that my clients felt secure in their wealth, now and in the future, so I received my Certified Retirement Planning Consultant (CRPC) designation.

All of this education and experience have taught me that it is critical to take the time to learn about the different needs of a business owner. There is no one-size-fits-all plan. Every business is different, and each aspect of your life, objectives, and needs will alter what the correct strategies are for you. Navigating financial jargon can be irritating, but we will be with you every step of the way in this book.

Chad Hrapmann: Wealth Advisor and co-Writer

I earned a Bachelor's degree in Civil Engineering at Louisiana State University and pursued an MBA degree at the University of New Orleans. At the beginning of my career, I applied my engineering and business management degrees in the oil and gas and industrial construction industries. My interest stems from its similarity to the problem-solving mindset in engineering but also from my exposure to the financial world in my early years. My dad, Bill Hrapmann, never steered his children's paths, but he was sure to educate us on finances in a practical way. For example, he used a portion of our earnings to contribute to a Roth IRA. These teachings tremendously helped improve my understanding of mutual funds, compounded interest, and many other financial investing elements. I feel that my engineering education has given me a different outlook on financial advising, which has helped serve what we at BHWA see as the most important aspect of our job: our clients.

You may be thinking, *I do not have time to learn all these terms; I am running my business.* This book was written with busy business owners in mind: you can skip ahead to the parts that most interest you. You can easily find relevant topics by skimming bulleted lists and finding the corresponding definitions in the margins. (To learn about the professionals who can help you achieve all your financial objectives, for example, skip ahead to Chapter 6.) Your potential savings are calculated in callout sections, and the objectives, pros, cons, and related professionals for strategies are listed beneath new financial concepts, when appropriate. Additionally, to help you stay focused as you read, there are simple *Action Steps* at the end of each chapter. Answer these questions to help you better understand your current finances and objectives to visualize a future in which your wealth grows and lasts.

This book will help you better understand wealth management and challenge you to think about how you can even better manage your income and estate taxes, protect your assets, and educate your heirs while setting them up for success. To be clear, this book does not render legal or tax advice on estate or income tax laws; the processes outlined in this book will instead guide you on decisions for your finances, so you can pursue the objectives that are important to you with the appropriate professionals.

No matter the size or value of your business, you can apply sound strategies to optimize your current and future finances. Taking the time to apply that attitude-of-success thinking to your financial picture will help you pursue what is personally important to you and your family and receive the benefits you deserve.

CHAPTER 1

WEALTH MANAGEMENT FOR BUSINESS OWNERS

Wealth management for business owners is different from those who do not garner the same level of wealth. Business owners are in total control of their wealth, from their retirement plans to their business strategies. The non-business owner does not have access to those decisions. You have all this power at your fingertips, but you could be squandering the opportunity. Reviewing the concepts in this chapter and strategies in the chapters to come can assist you even more in maintaining and managing your wealth.

As a business owner, there are many unique strategies to save income and estate taxes, expand and diversify your assets, and plan for your heirs. You have the opportunity to plan your future and pursue what is important to you. Many successful business owners take advantage of the more common strategies, such as utilizing 401(k)s, other salary deferrals, and owning company real estate and renting it back to the company. In later chapters, this book will review the common areas, the more advanced areas, and the correct financial tools to consider.

The most important aspect of **wealth management** for business owners is determining what is important to you and your family and what your objectives are. Whether you have been in business for many years or your business is new, whether you have hundreds of employees, or fewer than a dozen, you most likely have a vision for your future. Typically, your main focus as a successful business owner is minimizing taxes, growing your assets, and taking care of your heirs. Later chapters will cover these subjects in detail.

As a business owner, you may feel you are too busy to address or implement many of these subjects. You are busy with your business, and staying focused on building said business is how you became so successful. Regardless, make time to review your wealth and your essential objectives. This should be a top priority for you. It is important to consider this book as an extension of that focus, but to make learning new concepts easier, you can just skim this book for the strategies that most interest you and refer to your specialized professional on your Optimal Financial Team.

You have spent years building your legacy and deserve financial security and independence, so spend a minimum amount of time maximizing your efforts. Once you have finished, you can pass it on to your Optimal Financial Team to pursue the concepts further, and they can determine which strategies may benefit you.

OPTIMAL FINANCIAL TEAM

Can someone manage their own wealth and get by? Yes, of course, but this can lead to many missed opportunities and/or risks that could be avoided. You grew your wealth from growing a business, not being the middleman between your financial professionals. Knowing the correct questions to ask, which information is relevant, and applying the proper strategies or investment tools to suit your and your family's objectives is not going to be your expertise, nor should it. Successful business owners are great at using outside resources where needed to leave their main focus on the business's primary products or services. When it comes to wealth management, this should be no different. Ask yourself, *Who can accomplish this?* not, *How can I?*

WHAT IS AN OPTIMAL FINANCIAL TEAM?

The super-rich ($500 million +) have the need and resources to keep their financial professionals in-house on salary, working through the ins and outs of managing the family's legacy. This in-house team of experts is referred to as a "family office." These professionals on an expensive salary—$500,000–$1 million–salaries—are needed. Covering daily and long-term financial and legal tasks for the super-rich can be an extremely complex and ongoing matter.

The resources and technologies available today have allowed families, who may not be in the super-rich category, to collaborate and maintain a similar financial planning setup, just without the on-salary staff.

An Optimal Financial Team can be summarized as the full collaboration and communication among your financial professionals. The term "team" here is not necessarily a legal agreement on who will be working together but more of a mindset of collaboration to encourage among your financial professionals.

Open communication is one of the main aspects of creating this Optimal Financial Team. Become familiar with the professionals you work with, introduce them to each other, have conference calls, and continue to include relevant professionals as needed. Taking advantage of each financial professional's knowledge and expertise in an open-communication setting will uncover opportunities and gaps you may not have even considered. This is nothing against your knowledge in your business or personal assets, investments, and estate planning. But experience and daily workings in these financial, tax, or legal professions are needed to fully understand these strategies, know what questions to ask, and accomplish a client's objectives.

Your Optimal Financial Team Framework

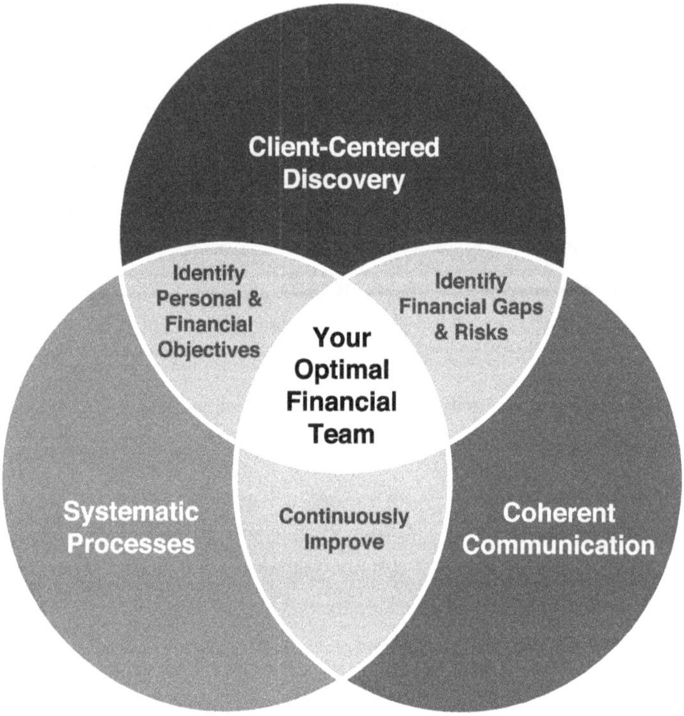

Bill Hrapmann Wealth Advisor, Inc. often meets with business owners with groups of trusted advisors, CPAs, attorneys, etc. However, the missing element is coordinating these advisors to develop a plan to meet the business owner's objectives. We come in and review the current state of the business owner's wealth and objectives to then meet with their current trusted advisors as a team. From there, we each work towards implementing our parts of your advanced plan.

WEALTH MANAGEMENT REVIEW

Business owners have a unique opportunity to explore financial strategies. Before you read about the tax, asset, and heir strategies in Chapters 2–5, it is important to ensure your finances are healthy enough to implement new strategies for your objectives. Here are some wealth management considerations that can help you identify potential issues in your finances or make your finances even better:

- Business vs. Personal Assets
- Business vs. Personal Objectives
- Constructive Destruction

BUSINESS VS. PERSONAL ASSETS

Business asset: an asset that exists within the business structure; an asset that a business owner has to aid them in the maintenance and growth of their business.

Personal asset: a piece of property or stock that aids an owner in their personal financial endeavors, not their business endeavors.

Many business owners co-mingle their business and personal assets. You have wealth beyond your business, so separate your assets to have a clearer picture of your finances and better determine whether your current strategies need to be changed and how those alternative strategies may benefit you.

Insist that your wealth advisor review these options with you and make a point of separating your business and personal assets.

Wealth advisors often work with business owners in these initial steps. Their expertise sets up the process to deliver meaningful, measurable results to guide you on preparation for the future.

Ensure your financial survival in case of unstable times ahead. You may need your personal investments to carry you and your family financially if the business cannot.

When you separate your company assets from your personal assets, this is how the two lists might look:

Business Assets	Personal Assets
Company building	Personal residence
Company real estate	Personal vehicles
Equipment	Family heirlooms
Company vehicles	Investments
Customer base	
Inventory	

Family heirlooms and customer bases would not be mixed—it is easy to see where those go, but others you may be tempted to see as one asset, when they should be designated to one area or the other.

If you tie up all your assets into your business, then you may be in a tough financial situation in the future. What if your business does not bring in the profit you expect it to over the next twenty years? Avoid this potential nightmare scenario by separating your assets, not only in a list but in practice. Consult with your wealth advisor about how to do this.

BUSINESS VS. PERSONAL OBJECTIVES

Business objectives, increasing profitability, rightfully come first. How you do that will vary based on your industry. However, it is still important to consider personal financial objectives, such as real estate, vehicles, retirement plans, education expenses, and investments, as they can keep you afloat in trying times, such as constructive destruction, which will be covered shortly.

Personal objectives do not need to be aligned with the objectives of your business. For instance, a personal objective might be buying a vacation home in a dream destination, while a business objective might be to earn $20 million annually and hire three new management staff members for expansion.

Setting a specific objective for yourself helps you plan out all your desires, such as acquiring a vacation home: consult with a real estate agent, research the neighborhoods that best meet your needs, and consider the home amenities you need in order to fulfill the objective you have been visualizing. Having a clear and specific target list helps you set objectives that are both achievable and realistic.

For those who are looking forward to luxurious retirements, setting objectives now helps you reach your objectives when the time comes. To do this, meet with your wealth advisor and other relevant financial professionals. (You will read about all manner of professionals in Chapter 6.)

By focusing separately on your personal and business objectives, you can set yourself up for success in both areas.

CONSTRUCTIVE DESTRUCTION

Constructive destruction is the systematic replacement of outdated products and services with new technology, making entire industries obsolete. Suddenly, a competitor has found a way to offer your service or product with a different unique selling proposition. Are there more prominent players that could steal your customers?

While constructive destruction is frightening for your business, it improves functionality for society as a whole. People do not want to go back to using pay phones or hailing taxis. The new systems in place benefit society better.

An excellent example of this phenomenon is Uber taking customers away from taxis in main cities. Do you think taxi companies ever saw this coming? You may not be able to see this kind of disruption coming. You must prepare your wealth for the unexpected. One way to protect your wealth is to build up *your* personal assets.

What has happened to camera stores, maps, taxis, and travel agents? They have all been rendered scarce or obsolete by the latest innovations. Whatever business you are in, look ahead to how technology and advancements might change your industry, and diversify to protect yourself and the company from constructive destruction.

If you are a camera manufacturer, then your sales have likely gone down with the advent of the iPhone and other smartphones. If you own a map company, then smartphones have also led to a decrease in sales due to the convenience of GPS applications.

When was the last time you or someone you know used a payphone? They no longer exist because of the rise of the cell phone. If you owned a business of payphone locations, your business has been completely replaced by technology. This is a prime example of constructive destruction.

Evaluate where you stand as a business: what industry are you in, and how do you diversify growth or sell sooner than later? Do not wait for technology to rob your company of its value. Stay ahead of the game. If you can foresee future demise in your industry, you can make better decisions by overcoming your emotions and seeing the big picture. You have got to sit down and think, *Where will the income come from?* Right now, you may not know. Wealth management will help you evaluate this type of constructive destruction for your own business and how you can either diversify, grow, or sell to minimize catastrophic loss and maximize value.

Mr. Hrapmann: Constructive Destruction Survivor

In the 1970s, dry cleaners did not predict the impact permanent press and polyester materials would have on their profits. It was devastating to the industry.

My father owned a dry-cleaning business in the '50s through the '70s. In the 1970s, permanent press and polyester clothing all but wiped out the dry-cleaning industry. No one in the industry could have foreseen this.

Fortunately, my father diversified his income. He was also an accountant, so he could continue generating revenue as a professional accountant through the '90s. His dry-cleaning business went under, but his income was able to survive the constructive destruction.

PRIORITIZE WEALTH MANAGEMENT

Be aware that getting a wealth management strategy in place takes effort. However, consider it a part of running your business; it is *that* vital. Making the effort to get the process started, and committing to following through, is something you will have to be intentional about. You may delegate some of the processes to your Optimal Financial Team, but you still have to be an active participant in the process.

The next chapter on income taxes is the first step of the wealth management process for business owners in achieving what is important to you and your family.

ACTION STEPS

Take a few minutes to gather a generalized list of your personal assets:

___

Do the same for your business assets:

___

What are your top three business objectives?

___

What are your top three personal objectives?

___

From our experience, this list can initially be generalized; it does not have to be detailed.

If you have questions or need more information, reach out to Bill Hrapmann Wealth Advisor, Inc by emailing info@billhrapmann.com.

CHAPTER 2

INCOME TAX STRATEGIES FOR BUSINESS OWNERS

Taxes are complicated, especially when you own a business. Just as owning a successful business adds additional steps in the tax-filing process, so too does it provide additional opportunities to minimize your taxes. On the federal level, there are three distinct and separate tax systems to consider for planning: the income tax system, the estate and gift tax system, and the generation-skipping tax system. Each requires substantial planning and knowledge to fully capitalize on available tax savings. This chapter focuses on the first and often most recognized: income taxes.

Before you read about specific strategies, however, it is important to recognize your different sources of income and how they are taxed. Any increase to your wealth, from whatever source, is in some way constituted as income and open to taxation. Income can be broken into three different categories:

- Active "Ordinary" Income
- Portfolio Income
- Passive Income

Active "Ordinary" income is income obtained from salary and wages associated with business or trade activities. If you are active on a daily basis and it is your main source of income, then that is most likely categorized as Active "Ordinary" income. On the federal level, active income is taxed at an increasing scale ranging from 10–37%, depending on your level of income.

Portfolio income is income coming from your investment portfolio in the shape of interests, dividends, and/or capital gains. Portfolio income is generally taxed as long-term gains and qualified dividends ranging from 0–28% depending on said gains.

Passive income comes in the form of real estate investments and conducting a trade or business in which you are not a material participant. Passive income has varying rules and definitions for which it can be taxed on the same scales as active income and/or portfolio income, depending on a multitude of different aspects.

The different aspects of income tax and income tax planning can be extremely comprehensive and complex with ever-changing federal, state, and even local laws. This chapter will not dive into the intricacies of the types of assets, methods of tax planning, types of real estate, or any other in-depth tax structuring. These specific items, all of which can affect your tax burden, are the reasons you, as a business owner, use a competent CPA that should know the intricate details of your unique business and income tax needs. This chapter will brush over the impacts of your income taxes based on your business structure and strategies designed to help lower your income tax burdens.

BUSINESS ENTITIES AND TAXATION

Prior to reading about specific income tax saving strategies, it is important to discern your corporate tax structure. The four types of business entities that will be covered, each with differences in tax structure, are:

1. Sole Proprietor
2. Partnership
3. Corporations
4. Limited Liability Company (LLC) (recognized by state)

SOLE PROPRIETORSHIP

Sole proprietorships are businesses owned and operated by a single individual (or husband and wife). The conditions that make up a sole proprietorship are engaging in a business or trade for profit and operating as yourself. You can operate a sole proprietorship under your name or under a trade or fictitious name, such as "Paul the Handyman." There are no filings required to operate as a sole proprietor but also no transfer of assets for protection since this entity is considered a legal extension of the individual.

Advantages

- Low cost and easy to form
- Simple to operate
- Easily sell business assets
- Little administrative burdens

Disadvantages

- Unlimited personal liability
- Income is subject to self-employment tax
- Generally low sources of capital
- No guarantee of continuity beyond proprietorship

PARTNERSHIPS

Partnerships are formed when two or more persons conduct a business as co-owners under their names or a trade name. If no other business entity is formed and two or more persons conduct a business together, a partnership is automatically created. There are many types of partnerships, which may be governed by different regulations, taxations, and liabilities. These differences will determine which partnership, if any, would work best for the interested parties and the manner they plan to conduct a business. Consult with a CPA and tax attorney to determine which partnership type best works for your situation.

Advantages

- More sources of capital than proprietorships
- Can be less complicated than corporations
- Income and losses are generally pass-through for tax purposes

Disadvantages

- Each partner is liable for the debts and obligations of the partnership
- All income is subject to payroll tax
- Selling partnership interests may be difficult

CORPORATIONS

Each business entity has its own set of benefits that may include generous tax breaks and asset protection. On the corporation level, there are two types of tax strategies to consider: the **C Corporation** and the **S Corporation.**

C Corporations

C Corporation: a tax designation in which the business owners or shareholders are taxed separately from the business itself.

C Corporations, under United States federal income tax law, are corporations taxed separately from their owners. However, the business profits may be taxed twice. Any excess profits for the C Corp get taxed first at the corporation level. Then, if the corporation paid out these profits as dividends, you are taxed on a personal level on these dividends. However, if you maintain profits to grow your business, the profits may be taxed lower in a C Corporation than in your personal tax return. The benefit is that the corporate tax bracket may be lower than your personal income tax bracket. (Important note: corporate taxation laws change periodically.) There are many other benefits to a C Corp structure, which you will want your tax experts to periodically review.

Advantages

- Limited liability to shareholders
- Unlimited number of owners (shareholders)
- Relative ease to raise capital
- Generally more management and tax savings resources
- Array of tax-advantaged strategies
- Corporate tax brackets may be lower than personal income tax

Disadvantages

- Double taxation potential
- Frequently changing laws
- More difficulty in forming and dissolving
- Administrative and registration burdens
- More complex filings and cash flow management when taking advantage of tax savings

S Corporations

S Corporation: a tax designation for both corporations and limited liability companies (LLCs) that enables business owners and shareholders to be taxed at one level of taxation.

Alternatively, you may structure your company as an S Corp. An **S Corporation**, as defined by Subchapter S of the tax code of the Internal Revenue Service (IRS), is a business entity with no more than one hundred shareholders that has elected to pass its corporate income, losses, credits, and deductions to its shareholders to include on their tax returns. With an S Corporation, there is no corporate tax. All profits are passed on to the S Corp owners, so you eliminate the double taxation which may have occurred in a C Corp. These S Corp profits are taxed at the shareholder's tax bracket. The tax cuts and JOBS Act of 2017 gave eligible S Corp shareholders a deduction of up to 20% of net qualified business income. Also, you may pass the losses of an S Corp through to the shareholders, who can use the losses to offset income (subject to tax law restrictions). However, a negative of having an S corporation is that if any profits remain in the company for expansion or equipment, the shareholders would be taxed on this profit even though they did not receive the profits, personally. This is called **phantom income** and is taxed on your personal income tax return even though you did not receive any payments.

Phantom income: profits that are taxed on your individual tax return that you did not receive.

Advantages

- Income is passed through to shareholders, avoiding double taxation
- Shareholders have limited liability
- Taxed at the individual level, which may be at a lower tax rate than the applicable corporate rate
- Certain distributions can be exempt from the payroll tax system

Disadvantages

- Limited to 100 shareholders
- Cannot have corporate or other certain trusts
- Tax rate at the individual level may be higher than the applicable corporate rate
- Borrowing may be difficult without stockholders' personal guarantees
- Shareholders owning more than 2% must pay taxes on employee fringe benefits, would possibly be tax-free in a C Corp

LIMITED LIABILITY COMPANIES (LLC)

Limited Liability Companies, or LLCs, are separate legal entities formed by one or more individuals in much the same way as corporations. The formation of LLCs is set in the document of Articles of Organization, and the ownership percentages are usually determined by the owners' contributions into the LLC. Relatively low formation costs and the ability to separate liabilities from personal assets are some of the main reasons LLCs are so popular. LLCs can also be used to separate assets, such as vacation homes, in the asset protection realm.

Advantages

- Owners (members) have limited liability
- Income is passed through, usually on a K-1 form
- Double taxation is avoided with the pass-through
- Multiple ways to elect taxation as partnership, S Corp, or C Corp

Disadvantages

- Transfer of interests may be difficult
- Laws vary from state to state regarding LLCs

- Some industries/professions are not permitted to operate under an LLC
- Laws are relatively new for LLCs, subject to changes and disadvantages

You may have a C Corporation but choose to change it to an S Corporation, or vice versa. Have your CPA review these details with you to help you make an informed decision about your business.

As previously mentioned, many benefits are not listed here, which is why it is important to meet with your financial professionals. For anything relating to your company structure, you want to depend heavily on the counsel of your attorney and CPA.

STRATEGIES TO MITIGATE INCOME TAXES

As a successful business owner, you are most likely taking advantage of some of the more common income tax saving strategies already, but this chapter also reviews lesser-known advanced tax strategies. In the following pages, you will be introduced to tax planning strategies with the goal of saving you tens of thousands or even hundreds of thousands of dollars.

COMMON TAX ADVANTAGED STRATEGIES

- IRAs
- Roth IRA
- Roth IRA Conversion
- Qualified Plans
  - 401(k) Plans
  - Profit Sharing Plans
- Health Savings Account (HSA)

Here are some more advanced income tax strategies that can significantly impact your wealth.

ADVANCED TAX ADVANTAGED STRATEGIES

- Payroll Tax Strategies
- Captive Insurance Company
- Employee Stock Option Plan (ESOP)
- Donor-Advised Fund
- Cash Balance Plan

Depending on your business structure and industry, there may be other tax advantaged plans to consider, such as SIMPLE IRAs, SIMPLE 401(k) Plans, 457 Plans, SEP IRAs, and more. Consult with your wealth advisor on your retirement and income tax saving objectives to best pick a strategy that works for you.

COMMON INCOME TAX STRATEGIES

IRAS AND ROTH IRAS

You have most likely heard of IRAs and Roth IRAs through any number of personal finance or retirement conversations. **IRAs**, or Individual Retirement Accounts, are used to shelter current and/or future income from taxation. **Traditional IRAs** are funded with before-tax income, enabling your investments to grow tax-deferred and are only required to be withdrawn at age seventy-two or older, when the withdrawals will be taxed as ordinary income. **Roth IRAs** work in almost the exact opposite way to Traditional IRAs. Roth IRAs are funded with after-tax income, also enabling investments to grow tax-deferred, so any qualified withdrawals are income tax-free.

The **Roth IRA** contribution is non-deductible, and earnings are tax-deferred and tax-free upon qualified withdrawals. The problem with the Roth IRA is that the depositor is limited to contributing based on their modified adjusted gross income, and most business owners can only contribute the max, $7,000 per year, to this fund. Business owners with an adjusted gross income of $200,000 or more (joint) may not be able to contribute to a Roth IRA. However, keep reading, and you will see that the Roth IRA can benefit you in other ways.

A Roth IRA may be great for younger investors such as your children if they have earned income and expect to be in a higher tax bracket as they mature into their careers.

Review your plans with your CPA and wealth advisor.

Objective: to serve as long-term retirement savings.

Pros: allows qualified, tax-free withdrawals.

Cons: restrictions on contributions and withdrawals apply.[2]

Professionals: CPA, wealth advisor

ROTH CONVERSIONS

If you are in a position where you will not need the assets or income from your IRA consider doing a **Roth Conversion** to pass on tax-free money to your next generation. With a Roth Conversion, you are converting your IRA to a Roth IRA and paying the income tax now in exchange for future tax-free qualified withdrawals. If you are under sixty years of age (specifically fifty-nine and six months), you should pay the taxes with non-retirement monies. You can convert your entire IRA as a whole or portions of your IRA at any time. The earlier the conversion the better, to allow the tax-free growth to make up on the loss due to taxes you paid today. Roth Conver-

2 Withdrawals of earnings prior to fifty-nine and a half or prior to the account being opened for five years, whichever is later, may result in a 10% IRS penalty tax. Limitations and restrictions may apply.

sions should especially be considered if you are in a lower income tax bracket in any particular year. Traditional IRA account owners have considerations to make before performing a Roth IRA conversion. These primarily include income tax consequences on the converted amount in the year of conversion, withdrawal limitations from a Roth IRA, and income limitations for future contributions to a Roth IRA. In addition, if you must take a required minimum distribution (RMD) in the year you convert, do so before converting to a Roth IRA.

QUALIFIED PLANS

Qualified plans offer tax advantages to employers and employees who maintain and participate in these plans. The purpose is to encourage retirement savings by both the employer and employee. As a business owner, you can take full advantage of both retirement savings and advantages on income taxes being the plan sponsor. Each plan requires specific design and maintenance to stay approved by the government. For this reason, consult with your wealth advisor along with your CPA when deciding to begin or change a current plan.

401(k)s

401(k) plans are grouped in the deferred contribution category, permitting contributions on a pre-tax basis reducing participants' current income tax liability. When beginning these plans, employers have options such as contribution matching at certain percentages of employee salaries, profit sharing, vesting options, along with many more. These plans offer employers the advantages of providing tax advantaged retirement savings to employees with minimum expenses along with the ability for the owners to also participate in the tax advantaged savings.

Profit Sharing Plans

Profit-sharing plans are established and maintained by employers to allow employees participation in the company's profits. Similar to other plans, these have specific regulatory and maintenance requirements to be accepted as a qualified plan to the government. These profit-sharing plans are another way to take advantage of tax deferred savings and also provide your company with an advantage over other companies who do not participate in the sharing of their profits.

HEALTH SAVINGS ACCOUNT (HSA)

Health Savings Accounts pay for qualified medical expenses with before tax dollars. HSAs are also triple tax-advantaged: tax-deductible contributions, tax-deferred growth, and tax-free withdrawals for qualified expenses. Consider not using this account for current medical expenses. Instead, let the account investments accumulate. If you keep all of your qualified medical receipts from the time this HSA was opened, you could have a large tax-free withdrawal that also grows tax-deferred in the future. Lastly, there is no required distribution at any time, unlike IRAs. To be qualified to contribute to an HSA, you must have a High Deductible Health Plan.

ADVANCED TAX ADVANTAGED STRATEGIES

PAYROLL TAX STRATEGIES

As a business owner, you match the employees' social security and Medicare tax on salary up to the social security wage base. The social security wage base in 2022 is $147,000.

The social security tax is 6.2%, and the Medicare tax is 1.45% on payroll up to the wage base. The Medicare tax does not have an income cap, so the salaries above the social security wage base continue to pay the 1.45% Medicare tax as the business owner. On your salary, you pay both the employee portion and the employer portion. The Social Security tax is 12.4% and the Medicare tax on your salary is 2.9%, at the time of this writing. Then, there is an additional tax of 0.9% on wages over $200,000 (single) or $250,000 (joint).

Review the necessary salary and determine whether taking profits will save you payroll taxes with your CPA. (In this example, you have $1 million of income from your business.) If you structure your business as an S Corp, you could save some of this payroll tax by taking profits instead of an excess salary. Consider having your salary up to the income limit for your retirement plan. In 2022, this limit is $305,000. You may be able to take the additional $695,000 as S corp profits, which could save you approximately $26,410 in Medicare taxes and high-income payroll taxes. However, there are industries where this strategy would not work. It is best to check with your CPA to stay current with this strategy and whether it is available in your industry.

If your children do some work around the business, you have potential tax savings available. By paying your children a lower salary than your own, you may put them in a much lower tax bracket. Their salary could be used to pay some of their expenses you are currently paying (for example, tuition, auto insurance, allowance, etc.). Then, with any leftover salary, your children could contribute to a Roth IRA. Qualified withdrawals from the Roth IRA are tax-free for retirement income if you make a withdrawal after you are fifty-nine and a half years old. Think about the value of compounded earnings for fifty years or longer, tax-free. If you are interested in pursuing this route, you will want to review with your CPA and wealth advisor.

There are strategies to pay yourself and/or your family the same income but with less payroll and/or income tax.

CAPTIVE INSURANCE COMPANY

Captive insurance company: a type of insurance that provides risk-mitigation and tax-advantaged strategies for any out-of-pocket deductions or to cover unique risk not covered by the standard insurance policy.

One of the most unique benefits business owners have to take advantage of is the captive insurance policy. A captive insurance policy is designed for the business owner to cover risks that traditional insurance may not cover. Premiums are paid into this policy, and these funds are available if claims arise for those unique risks. This is an opportunity to use these insurance reserves to invest and grow your wealth before it is possibly used for insurance purposes.

If you have your own **captive insurance company**, you pay insurance premiums to your insurance company instead of paying those premiums to a commercial insurance company. Now, you can save and invest those premiums to be used in the event of the covered insurance risk or to grow your wealth if there is never a claim. Suppose your captive insurance company covers an insurable risk such as fire or health insurance for employees. In that case, you can add co-insurance through your regular commercial insurance carrier at a discounted rate since you are covering the first dollars of risk. The premiums would be deducted at ordinary income tax rates and potentially grow tax-free, so at the sale or closing of your company, you can withdraw the remaining balance (which could be millions of dollars) at the **capital gain tax rate.** Currently, the maximum capital gain tax rate is 20% plus 3.5% health care tax for a total of 23.5%. Compare this to your ordinary income tax bracket, which may be as high as 37%.

Capital gains tax rate: the amount of taxes you pay

depending on the length of time that you hold a capital asset before selling it.

You may make deductible contributions to your captive insurance company and then invest those contributions to accumulate and grow. Your insurance provider would pay any claims arising from the risks defined in the captive insurance policy from this fund.

Well-informed wealthy people use captive insurance companies to cover uncommon risks. Many restaurants in 2020 did not have insurance covering a mandatory closure because of the COVID-19 pandemic, but a business owner with a captive insurance company covering this risk could have made a claim and received a tax advantage benefit. The policy would have had to be in place for many years to accumulate enough reserves to cover any claims. A business owner facing similar threats of closure in the future may want to create their own captive insurance company to cover losses from such an event.

Many businesses begin with coverage on the deductible or self-insured portions of general liability, automobile insurance, property and casualty insurance, and working compensation losses. They then expand the coverage to cover unique risks that may include management liability, environmental liability, and other risks unique to your industry.

Upon selling or closing your company, under current rules, you may withdraw the balance in this captive insurance company as long-term capital gains, which are typically taxed much lower than ordinary income tax rates.

Objective: to cover uninsured risk or lower premiums on insurable risk.

Pros: double premiums, investment of premium, tax benefits add withdrawal.

Cons: maintaining the captive insurance company, building up capital.

Professionals: insurance agent, CPA, tax attorney, wealth advisor.

Your Potential Savings: Captive Insurance Company

Elliot paid $2 million of premiums to his captive insurance company over the years and deducted these premiums at a 40% tax rate, saving $800,000 in taxes.

Because there were no claims, his invested premiums grew to $5 million. As of 2021 tax rules, he was able to close his company and pay 20% capital gain rates on the $3 million–gain (from $2 million to $5 million), which is $600,000, plus 3.5% healthcare tax total.

The estimated net income after taxes into his captive insurance company was $1.2 million ($2 million in premiums minus $800,000 in tax savings), and the net coming out of his captive insurance company was $4.4 million ($5,000,000 minus $600,000 in taxes).

EMPLOYEE STOCK OPTION PLANS (ESOP)

An **Employee Stock Option Plan (ESOP)** is an employee benefit plan which gives a business owner, such as yourself, an option to sell company shares to the plan (employees) and receive various income and estate tax savings. This stock ownership incentive also encourages employees to better participate in the growth and appreciation of the company, since they also become shareholders. Not only do these plans help motivate and align employee interests with that of the company, but the tax benefits for the business owner can be a great reason to look into implementing an ESOP. Consult with your CPA, tax attorney, and wealth advisor to determine whether an ESOP is suitable for your business.

DONOR-ADVISED FUND

> **Donor-advised fund:** an investment fund, created by an organization, that is typically administered by a third-party and allows the donor to make tax-deductible contributions and maintain control over the distribution of the donations to qualified charities.

A **donor-advised fund** is of maximum benefit when you are in a high tax bracket and want to make a substantial charitable contribution but do not want the charity to receive the contribution all at once, or you are undecided on the charities to which you want to contribute. This flexibility to choose the charity later gives you the advantage of tax deductions now and the ability to choose your charity each year, whether your views have changed or the charity's values have.

If you have an interest in charitable contributions, consider a donor-advised fund while you are in a high tax bracket (either from general income or the sale of your business). With a donor-advised fund, you do not have to decide the charity until you want the fund to make a distribution.

Objective: to enable tax savings through charity contribution.

Pros: tax savings now; you may wait to decide the charitable beneficiary.

Cons: the gift is irrevocable.

Professionals: CPA, wealth advisor.

CASH BALANCE PLAN

Cash balance plan: a type of retirement plan that calculates benefits based on a formula that takes into account various factors.

Most likely, your company has a defined contribution pension plan such as a profit-sharing, 401(k) salary deferral plan, or a combination profit-sharing 401(k) plan. A defined contribution plan defines the contribution. For example, you may pay 10% of company payroll into a defined contribution plan or to a 401(k) plan, matching 4% of deferred salaries for the employees who participate. Plans such as these may be necessary to retain top-quality employees in your industry. If your company only has a few employees, as the highly compensated business owner, you may even be paying less into the plan for your employees than you are saving in taxes.

You may recall the **defined benefit pension plan**, prevalent thirty to forty years ago. In a defined benefit pension plan, an actuary determines the benefit of a "retirement income" or pension. To fund this future benefit, employers made expensive annual contributions determined by the plan's investment performance, employee salaries, and their age. This unknown future contribution for the employer made future cash flow uncertain, so most companies converted to a defined contribution plan such as the profit-sharing and 401(k) salary deferral. In these defined contribution plans, the employer could choose the contribution amount each year.

Now, the **cash balance plan** (a type of defined benefit plan) is not the same as the old defined benefit plan mentioned above. In the traditional profit-sharing 401(k), you as a highly compensated business owner are limited to contributing approximately $50,000 a year for yourself. With the cash balance defined benefit pension plan, you may be able to contribute more than $250,000 per year for yourself. That is five times more of a deductible contribution and possibly very little more than you have already been contributing for your employees.

We often work with business owners who already have qualified plans in place, but not everyone does. In the following real-world example, this business owner has a profit-sharing plan in place. We analyzed the benefits of adding a cash balance plan to further assist this business owner's income tax savings and retirement planning.

This is a hypothetical example and is not representative of any specific situation. Your results will vary. The hypothetical rates of return used do not reflect the deduction of fees and charges inherent to investing.

In this example, the business owner can add an additional $291,000 to his own tax deferred retirement savings while only being required to increase his employee contributions by $15,000. For simplistic reasons, presume the business owner's tax rate is around 40%, common among many successful business owners. That $291,000 of what would be taxable income would only equate to $174,600 of after-tax income.

Using this cash balance plan with his profit-sharing plan, he is able to save the total $291,000 as tax-deferred

Comparing Profit Sharing & Cash Balance Plan

COMPANY DEMOGRAPHICS

	Participants	Age	Estimated Compensation
Business Owner	1	64	$290,000
# of Non-Owner HCE	10	28 – 59	$130,000 – $290,000
# of Non-HCE	12	25 – 50	$40,000 – $110,000

RETIREMENT PLAN COMPARISON

Participant	Profit Sharing Contributions	Cash Balance & Profit Sharing Contributions	Difference
Business Owner	$29,000	$320,000	+ $291,000
Non-Owner HCE	$120,000	$130,000	+ $10,000
Non-HCE	$60,000	$65,000	+ $5,000
Total	**$209,000**	**$515,000**	**+ $306,000**

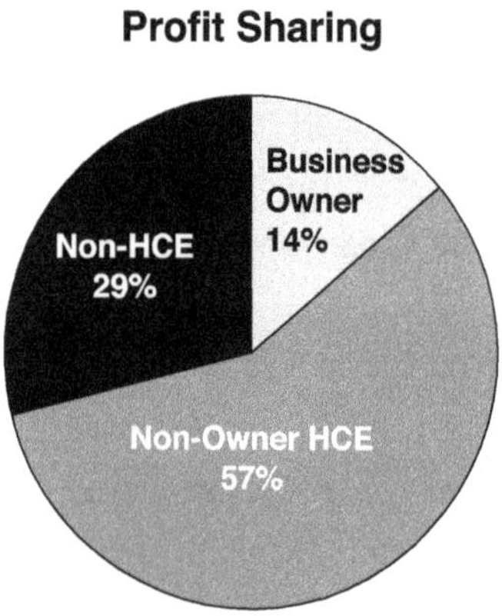

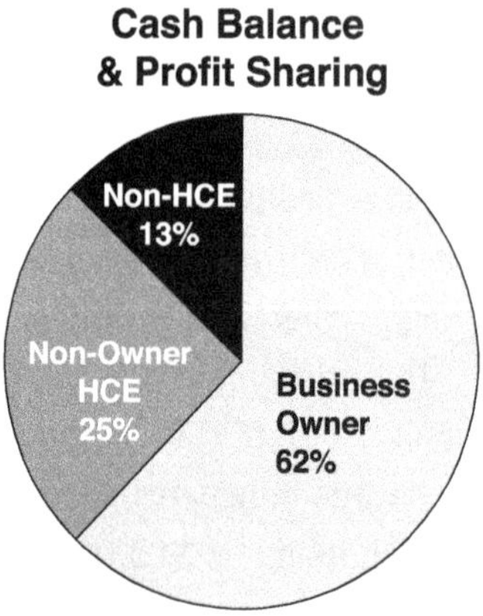

investments and avoid an additional $116,400 of taxes. The owner is also providing additional retirement savings, the sum of $15,000, to his employees on monies that would have likely been lost to taxes. Cash balance plans can be a powerful income tax mitigating tool under the right circumstances.

This cash balance plan has a few qualifying rules and regulations. It typically works for business owners who are fifty years old or older and have fewer than thirty employees. To determine whether this will work for you, contact your wealth advisor and the third-party administrator of your current plan to ask for a review.

Consult with your wealth advisor to analyze whether the cash balance plan may be the right financial tool for you.

Objective: to maximize tax deductible contributions for the owner.

Pros: substantially increasing the owner's contribution while not (or minimally) increasing the contributions for employees.

Cons: increasing administrative cost to maintain plan commitment for three to five years or longer to fund this plan.

Professionals: CPA, wealth advisor.

SAVE MORE ON INCOME TAXES

As a business owner, your finances are complicated. You are in control of deciding on strategies to implement that can make you and your family even more prepared and protected for the future. There are more professionals involved. With the help of a wealth advisor, CPA, attorney, and other specialized professionals, you have many opportunities to coordinate your personal objectives with the future of your business.

ACTION STEPS

Consider which company tax structure would be most beneficial for your business.

Which income tax strategies would you be interested in learning more about?

If you have questions or need more information, reach out to Bill Hrapmann Wealth Advisor, Inc by emailing info@billhrapmann.com.

CHAPTER 3

ESTATE TAX STRATEGIES FOR BUSINESS OWNERS

At one point or another, you have to accept the fact that you will not be around forever. As with many business owners, you will most likely leave a wide range of assets and wealth to your spouses, heirs, charities, or anyone else you so choose. Are both you and your spouse familiar with your family's estate tax plan? Are your children mature enough to inherit your estate and preserve your legacy? Will there be assets left over for your grandchildren's education and future?

These are questions to ask yourself, not in a judgmental or doubtful way but to reveal how important it is to have strategies in place for your estate. It took a lifetime for you to grow this wealth, so do your part to protect it for generations to come. Along with most parts of your life, your hobbies, passions, and beliefs are unique to you—and so are your intentions for your estate. Generally, the objectives for estate planning come down to the following:

- Transfer wealth and assets as desired with minimum estate taxes due
- Use lifetime gifting exclusions to save taxes

- Plan for children
- Prepare for incapacity on financial and medical decisions
- Provide for spouse's needs
- Fulfill charitable intentions

Before getting into these specific objectives, you may be asking yourself, *What exactly is an estate?* Most if not all business owners have heard of estates, heirs, and inheritance, but you may not have sat down and looked at your estate as a whole to plan for when you are no longer around.

Your estate is made up of everything you own or partially own, including both personal and business assets. These assets are broken into two categories, **Probate** and **Non-Probate**. Probate assets are assets in your name but do not, or cannot, have a named beneficiary, and go through the probate process to get to the next owner. This includes business entities, real estate, non-retirement investment accounts, bank accounts, vehicles, and more. Non-Probate assets are assets held with beneficiary designations or assets in trusts. There can be many non-probate assets, but the more common assets with beneficiary designations include your 401(k), IRAs, life insurance policies, and annuities.

Assets that do not have a beneficiary designation will use your Last Will and Testament through a probate court process to be distributed to your heirs. This process may take six months or longer to complete. Does your spouse have enough liquid assets to get through this process?

There are basic documents to consider for estate planning but with the complexities of estate planning it is recommended you discuss all of your objectives with an estate attorney and your wealth advisor.

- Wills
- Powers of attorney
- Durable powers of attorney for healthcare and finances

- Living wills or advanced medical directives
- Do not resuscitate orders

Currently, the taxable portion of your estate may be taxed at 40%. That means every $1 million in your estate may be taxed at $400,000. Thankfully, you may use an **exemption equivalent** to exempt up to $12.06 million from estate taxes per person as of 2022. A married couple may have $24.12 million non-taxed estate through the exemption equivalent.

> **Exemption equivalent:** the amount in assets which can be passed estate or gift tax-free.

However, this $12.06 million–exemption equivalent will sunset in 2026 to $5 million per person. It is unknown how regulations will change the exemption equivalent in the coming years, which is why it is important to get clear on the value of your estate and decide the financial tools to use to minimize your estate taxes.

As a business owner, you may take many avenues to better control your wealth and the amount you pay in taxes. You may utilize specific strategies in your business that give you estate tax deductions, minimize the value of gifting company shares to your children, and open different, relevant trusts.

In the previous chapter, you learned that choosing the right business structures, implementing cash flow strategies, and various retirement plans can help minimize your income tax burden. To minimize *estate* taxes, you may have to give up ownership or assets so that they will no longer be included in your estate.

WHEN YOU DIE, WHAT HAPPENS?

When a person dies, their surviving heirs inherit a lengthy to-do list. The disbursement of financial and sentimental assets to the descendants of one's estate can be a harrowing process. Certain ownership types are transferred automatically to a surviving spouse, joint owner, or a named beneficiary. For assets that are not, there is the **probate process**, in which a decedent's assets are transferred to their heirs by contract or law and retitled into the heirs' names. This can be summed up as the legal processing and validity of your last will and testament. If the decedent did not establish a last will and testament, the state in which they are domiciled has a set of laws that will be followed to transfer these assets to their heirs. Do not give the state complete control over who gets which assets from your estate; create a current will and have it reviewed every three to five years by your Optimal Financial Team.

The probate process has some advantages in that the legal proceedings will, for the most part, follow the wishes and desires of your will. The other advantage is these legal proceedings provide for an orderly administration of the decedent's assets.

STRATEGIES TO MITIGATE ESTATE TAXES

Mitigating estate taxes is both an art and science. Blending several strategies and coordinating among your estate attorney, CPA, and wealth advisor is of the utmost importance in estate planning. The following strategies are only an introduction to some well-known strategies; more advanced and complex strategies will go beyond the scope of this book. Working closely with your Optimal Financial Team will allow your estate to be reviewed in greater detail and determine whether any advanced strategies suit your needs and objectives.

Here are some estate tax strategies to minimize your estate taxes:

- A Properly-Drafted Will
- Exemption Equivalent
- Utilizing Trusts

- › Residence Trust
- › Intentionally Defective Grantor Trust
- › Charitable Remainder Trust
- › Charitable Lead Trust
- › Irrevocable Life Insurance Trust (ILIT)
- › Dynasty Trusts
- Gifting

A PROPERLY-DRAFTED WILL

If there is one statement that cannot be overstated, it is this: you must create and maintain a properly-drafted will that is in line with your wishes and intentions after your death. This document, bar none, is an essential part of any estate plan. A will is a legal document that allows the creator to control the distribution of their assets and the ability, in general, to avoid a state's distribution laws for those without a will. Wills may be amended or revoked by the creator and are not implemented until their death. In short, a will can be thought of as a voice of the decedent directing how probate assets should be handled and distributed among heirs.

Wills allow you to select how and where your probate assets are distributed. They also help maximize utilization of any marital deduction, implement provisions to minimize estate tax burdens, fulfill charitable intentions, and designate guardians for minor children. To properly draft a will, you must also understand the consequences of a will. This legal document will be interpreted and executed according to the writings in said will; your heirs will not be able to say, "It says this, but they actually meant this." Proper thought and discussion among you and your spouse are needed to create wills that follow your intentions. Use a series of *If this happens, then this should happen* questions to go through possible scenarios and wanted results.

At Bill Hrapmann Wealth Advisor, Inc. (BHWA), we find it helpful to draw a diagram of your initial thoughts to be shared with your attorney. Illustrating the wishes and objectives you have for your will can be extremely helpful to ensure all parties have a shared understanding.

"If I die first, what is needed to support my spouse? Should I guarantee my children any assets? Are my children mature enough to inherit this? Do I want to make sure my grandchildren have their education funded?"

These questions along with many more are the kinds you and your spouse will want to ask while planning out your wills.

Another very important consideration when drafting a will or a trust is picking the **executor** and **trustee**. This selection, often overlooked, needs to be thought about to a similar degree as the content in the will or trust itself. An **executor** is a personal representative appointed by the decedent to administer the estate according to the will. A **trustee**, trust administrator appointed by the trust document, is more involved and requires more active responsibilities. Your executor will be legally responsible for executing the instructions and wishes of your will, along with possibly maintaining and/or selling assets to fulfill these instructions.

Careful, unemotional consideration is required, especially if the executor will also be receiving inheritance. The trustee(s) of any trusts will have an ongoing responsibility until the trust assets are disbursed and the trust is closed. Another matter to be considered when choosing a trustee is compensation. Distributing, maintaining, and/or selling assets according to a will or trust can be a time-consuming job. Whoever you choose as your trustee should be compensated accordingly. This is just another incentive assuring the

wishes and instructions of these documents are carried out how you and your spouse intended.

EXEMPTION EQUIVALENT

As of early 2022, the estate and gift tax exemption equivalent is $12.06 million per person. A married couple with a properly drafted will could have an exemption of $24.012 million. However, remember that in 2026 there is a sunset provision which lowers the exemption equivalent down to $5 million per person or $10 million per couple if no legislative changes are made beforehand. This means that, excluding changes in 2022, the first $24.12 million is not taxed. This exemption amount can be changed anytime by any administration in office. While the exemption is high, consider utilizing this with gifts to heirs before the amount sunsets in 2026.

The federal estate tax started with the revenue act of 1916. Since then, there have been numerous changes to the exemption equiva-

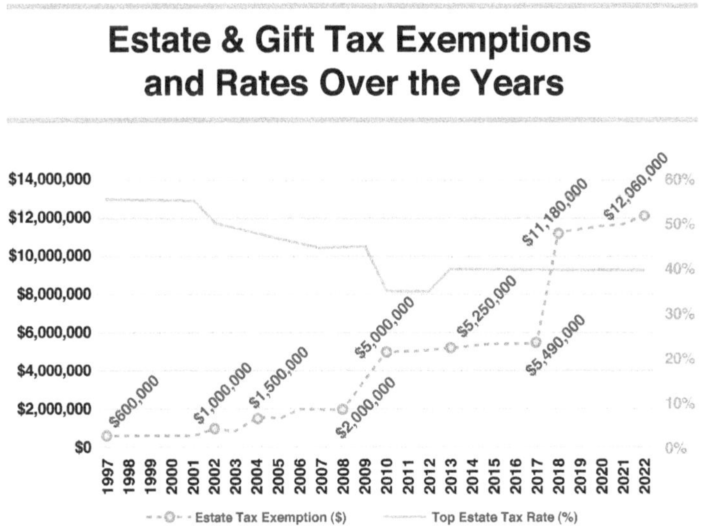

lent (including adding gift tax) and the tax percentage. Since 1997, the exemption equivalent has increased to its current value. Estate and gift taxes are calculated from the same exemption amount.

Even if not changed by an administration, this current estate tax law has a sunset provision in 2026, reverting to an exemption equivalent of approximately $5 million per person. Once you pass your exemption equivalent, the first $1 million is taxed at 18–39%. Any taxable value over $1 million is taxed at 40%. That is $400,000 per million. For a married couple, the unused exemption value is portable to the surviving spouse; however, you must first select this portability option on your estate tax return. Currently, any appreciated assets receive a stepped-up basis in your succession. See the explanation of the stepped-up basis below (though note that that stepped-up basis could be taken away as legislation changes). Your appreciated assets could be taxed with both estate taxes and capital gain taxes.

Also known as a step up in basis, a stepped-up basis is a type of readjustment that takes into account the fair market value of an asset at the owner's death (valuation date) or the value six months after the death date (alternative valuation date). This basis adjustment helps minimize capital gains tax. The alternative valuation date is provided to give relief to estates with a high value due to temporary market conditions.

Bonus Potential Savings: Stepped-up Basis

Imagine you made an investment of $100,000 in a stock, and it increased in value to $1 million. Upon the sale of this stock, depending on your tax filing bracket, you would owe capital gains tax on the $900,000 gain at the current capital gain rate of 20% plus 3.8% (Medicare surtax), which comes out to 23.8% capital gains tax.

This would amount to $214,200.

If the stock is not sold and remains part of your assets in your succession, the tax basis would increase to the present value at your death, which is $1 million in this example. Then, your heirs could sell this stock for this value and not owe any capital gains tax, even though you gained $900,000 in growth from your initial investment.

RESIDENCE TRUST

Residence trust: an irrevocable trust that allows the owner of a home to transfer their assets to a beneficiary to minimize estate taxes on the property.

A **residence trust** is an estate tax strategy that works well for wealthy people who own multiple houses. This trust enables you to gift your home to your children at a discounted value, so you can lower your estate. During an agreed-upon period, you can reside in the home without paying rent to your beneficiary. At the end of the term, however, you have to start paying rent to your children. The rent at fair market value, which is not a gift, also lowers your estate. Special calculations by your estate attorney will determine the value of your gift. You need to live beyond the rent-free timeframe to remove this property from your estate.

INTENTIONALLY DEFECTIVE GRANTOR TRUST

As of 2022 tax laws, trusts are taxed at a 37% income tax bracket on income greater than $13,450. To mitigate this tax, you could create an **Intentionally Defective Grantor Trust (IDGT)** for your child, so you could pay the income tax on the income in the trust, which lowers your estate and leaves the income in the trust for the beneficiaries.

> **Intentionally defective grantor trust:** an estate planning tool that freezes certain assets for estate tax purposes. By paying yearly income taxes on the assets, the trust income remains in trust (out of your estate) and the grantor pays the income tax which lowers their estate.

The grantor (the person who created the trust) would pay the income tax on the trust income, the defective part of the trust. The *asset* in the trust is recognized for estate tax purposes, but the *income* is still the grantor's income. This expense lowers the grantor's estate as well while leaving the trust to grow with the accumulated income or pay the income out to the beneficiaries.

Objectives: to remove an asset from the grantor's estate with future growth out of the estate as well.

Pros: lowers taxable estate, income from the asset will go to the trust.

Cons: the income from the asset is permanently given up.

Professionals: tax attorney, CPA.

CHARITABLE TRUSTS

Before choosing between the numerous types of charitable trusts, decide what you want to accomplish. Do you want a charity to receive income from an asset now and then have the asset passed to your heirs? Or would you prefer to receive the income now and then have the assets distributed to a charity after a certain time frame or at your death?

Charitable Remainder Trust (CRT) is a gift of cash or property to an irrevocable trust. The donor (you) receives an income stream from the trust for a term or for life, and the named charity receives the remaining trust assets at the end of the trust term.

Charitable Lead Trust (CLT) is a cash or asset gift to an irrevocable trust. A named charity receives an income stream from the trust for a term. After the income stream period ends, the remaining assets are distributed to the non-charitable beneficiaries, such as your heirs.

With either the charitable remainder trust or a charitable lead trust, you may receive income and/or estate tax benefits. Depending on the trust, you may continue to receive income, in which case the asset goes to a charity, or you can have a charity utilize the benefit of the asset, in which case the asset goes to your heirs.

Objective: To provide income or assets to a charity before or after you die.

Pros: Making contributions of income or an asset to a charity and utilizing the tax benefits.

Cons: Giving up the income or the asset.

Professionals: CPA, tax attorney.

IRREVOCABLE LIFE INSURANCE TRUST (ILIT)

> **Irrevocable Life Insurance Trust (ILIT):** a type of life insurance trust that can own and manage a life insurance policy while the insured is still alive. It can also distribute the proceeds after the insured's death.

You may have insurance policies that are no longer needed to support your surviving spouse. If you own a policy, the death benefit value is included in your estate. For example: if you have a $1 million–policy and your estate tax bracket is at 40%, $400,000 of this $1 million would go to estate taxes. By simply gifting this policy into an irrevocable life insurance trust (ILIT), the full $1 million–death benefit would go to your beneficiary of the ILIT without any estate taxes. There is a three-year waiting period for existing policies gifted into the irrevocable life insurance trust to be out of your estate. New life insurance policies applied for and owned by the trust are immediately out of your estate and will not have a three-year waiting period.

If your estate needs liquidity to continue the business or pay estate taxes, look into investing into a new policy inside of the ILIT. There are specialized cost-efficient survivorship policies to consider utilizing to pay your estate taxes or provide liquidity for your business. Review this with your wealth advisor.

Objective: to not have life insurance proceeds taxed in your estate.

Pros: easily done by transferring current policies or investing into new policies in this ILIT trust.

Cons: irrevocable, beneficiaries fixed.

Professionals: tax attorney, wealth advisor.

DYNASTY TRUSTS

Dynasty trusts are set up and designed to last for long periods, if not forever (unless state laws disallow perpetuities). These trusts are created to the extent that the assets are kept in the trust and are not directly distributed to the beneficiaries. The prime benefit of setting up a trust in this manner is the ability to avoid transfer taxation at the death of each generation moving forward. Instead, the gained income and/or interest can be used to provide for the beneficiaries. This allows the value of assets in the trust to be excluded from the gross estate of the beneficiaries.

Objective: to provide generational wealth for long periods.

Pros: avoid transfer taxations and exclusion from estate for each generation onward.

Cons: may not be perpetual, limited access/control of assets to heirs.

Professionals: tax attorney, wealth advisor.

GIFTING

Gifting is the gratuitous transferring of assets to another person during your life. The federal government has an implemented tax (the gift part of estate and gift taxes) on this giving to raise revenue. Before this gift tax, established in 1932, some individuals would transfer income-producing property to family members in a lower tax bracket to help reduce the family's overall income tax burden. With this gift tax implementation also came the estate, gift, and generation-skipping transfer exemptions you have today. These exemption amounts and laws surrounding them are in constant review, and changes can happen year to year. Discuss all of your gifting intentions with your wealth advisor to fully take advantage of the current exemptions.

You can gift any amount up to $16,000 per person per year in cash or assets without owing estate and gift tax. Because this amount is a gift, it is no longer considered part of your estate. However, if you gift more than $16,000, you will have to claim that excess amount against your exemption equivalent.

Suppose a married couple wants to give money to their child to buy a house. That is fine. (Education and medical expenses do not count as gifts.) However, if this amount is above the annual gift tax exclusion, $16,000 per person per year, then they would have to file a gift tax return. They will use part of their exemption equivalent amount (which changes depending on the administration).

You can gift other assets instead of cash that may equate to more value than $16,000. Business ownership, company stocks, or property are available to gift, which may have discounted value benefits. Discounting the value of gifts will be explained in the next section.

Gifting Company Shares

When gifting $2 million of shares of a publicly traded company, the full $2 million would be included in the gift calculation. However, if you are gifting $2 million of shares in your company and this $2 million of shares is 10% of the ownership of your company, the gift may receive a minority ownership discount in the gifting calculation. With a potential 30% discount on the gift, a savings of $600,000 of gift value would occur. At a 40% estate tax rate, this would be an initial $240,000 in estate tax savings. With potential future appreciation, this appreciation is also out of your estate. If these shares increase in value from $2 million to $6 million, you have potential estate tax savings of $1,600,000. If your business is an S Corporation, you must abide by other ownership rules to maintain the S Corporation status. Any profits (distributed or undistributed) would take place on the basis of ownership. In this example, 10% of profits would go to new owners.

As a precaution to maintain control, first, you may want to create **non-voting shares**, so you can give the non-voting shares and retain voting control of your company by keeping the **voting shares**. With both voting and non-voting shares, any profits distribute on a pro-rata basis.

If your company profits are $1 million and your children own 10% of the shares, they will receive $100,000 of the profit (for both cash profit distributions and phantom income, profits withheld to reinvest back into the company). Shareholders will owe income tax on the profits, whether distributed or not.

To further lower the value of your estate, consider utilizing an **Intentionally Defective Grantor Trust** to own the shares. In this case, the grantor pays the income tax on the profit distributions on the shares held in this trust, which also lowers your estate and increases the amount available in this trust (because the trust is not paying taxes; you are).

Voting shares: shares that give investors the right to vote on corporate decisions.

Non-voting shares: shares that do not have voting rights. They can be used by business owners to gift or sell shares without giving up any control of the business.

Objective: to lower estate taxes by transferring partial ownership and income from the company to your heirs.
Pros: by leveraging the gift of minority ownership shares you can maximize the value of the gift while minimizing the exemption equivalent used. The appreciation of these shares will not be included in your estate.
Cons: the gifted shares of the company and the pro-rata income are permanently given up.
Professionals: CPA, tax attorney, wealth advisor

Your Potential Savings: Gifting Shares and Minority Shareholders

Imagine John and Sue, a husband and wife, own 100% of their manufacturing company, and the business is growing. They currently have a taxable estate, meaning if they died, they would owe taxes on the amount of estate above the exemption equivalent ($24.012 million). They feel that the business will continue growing, and their estate taxes will increase. In that case, they can go ahead and gift a portion of the business to the next generation, before their tax liability increases even higher.

If they were to gift $1 million worth of minority non-voting shares to the next generation, the IRS may view the value of that gift, for gift tax purposes, as only $700,000 (after a 30% discount). If the business grows 10% per year for the next twenty years, the $1 million–gift would be worth $6–7 million when the couple dies. At a 40% estate tax bracket, this may save $2.4–2.8 million in estate taxes.

SAVE ON ESTATE TAXES

Review this valuation with your CPA and tax attorney before doing any in-depth estate planning. Do not have unrealistic valuation expectations (either too high or too low) when it comes to your estate; get it evaluated realistically so that you can decide estate planning strategies and minimize estate taxes. If you are in a position to be paying estate taxes, then perhaps now is an excellent time to give shares or assets to the next generation at discounted values while the exemption equivalent is $12.06 million per person.

ACTION STEPS

What is the estimated value of your taxable estate?

____

Which estate tax strategies do you feel would help meet your objectives?

____

If you have questions or need more information, reach out to Bill Hrapmann Wealth Advisor, Inc by emailing info@billhrapmann.com.

CHAPTER 4

ASSET PROTECTION

Assets are not only in danger of damage and losses from natural disasters but also of being unjustly taken from you through creditors, lawsuits, and too commonly, divorce. Protecting these assets can be done in various ways. Common ways to protect assets include using insurance policies, trusts, and different business entities. Keep your own precious assets in mind when reading the following story.

The Importance of Asset Protection

Natural disasters happen across the United States in varying forms such as earthquakes, tornados, or blizzards. On the Gulf Coast, hurricanes are the prevalent catastrophic events that become an annual threat between the months of June and November. On August 29, 2005, the infamous Hurricane Katrina made landfall, causing unthinkable damage to the Gulf Coast, which in some parts can still be seen to this day.

Our practice is located in southern Louisiana, so many clients' personal assets and/or business assets were affected to varying degrees. Two businesses in particular were passive in their dealings with their insurances and annual renewals. And who can blame them? They're busy running a business, making payroll, working toward growth, so insurance renewals are not at the top of the daily task list. Both business owners were under the assumption that they had flood insurance coverage. However, there was a communication gap somewhere along the way, and the business owner did not have flood insurance on their business buildings.

Put yourself in that situation: you assume you have coverage just to find out you now have to pay out of pocket to recover from this insurable event.

Unforeseen damage and losses will always be tough but not nearly as difficult as uncovered damage and losses. Open communication between you, your insurance agent, and your wealth advisor needs to be a priority when dealing with asset protection. Be sure your property and casualty agent is on your Optimal Financial Team.

Apart from the varying disasters throughout the country that each require more focus on particular coverages, there are also differences in laws among the states regarding asset protection. Many states have their own specific laws to protect assets, such as your residence, cash values of life insurances, retirement accounts, and annuities. This can be very complicated and not uniform from state to state, so the importance of open communication between your CPA, tax advisor, wealth advisor, insurance broker, and other financial experts is crucial when addressing asset protection. The provided information is for educational purposes only, and you should consult your professional experts on these matters.

STRATEGIES TO PROTECT YOUR ASSETS

Following, you will read about asset protection strategies using:

- Insurances
- Investment Vehicles
- Prenuptial Agreements
- Business Entities
- Trusts
- Buy-sell Agreements

INSURANCES

As a business owner, or as an heir yourself, you are likely familiar with various insurance coverages such as homeowner's insurance, liability insurance, and auto insurance. However, the details of insurance policies may not be of interest unless, of course, you have a claim. But at the end of the day, you most likely utilize these necessary insurances and accept the seemingly endless premiums for something you hope is never needed. You know that having the proper insurance coverage is a necessary part of maintaining your assets and protecting your wealth for you and the heirs to come.

There are many types of insurance to consider, but these are the types you will read about in this section:

- Property-casualty insurance
- Umbrella policy
- Specialty Insurances

Get protected *before* a loss or a claim. You always want protection on your assets from the very beginning.

Property-casualty Insurance

> **Property-casualty insurance:** insurance covering various types of assets and liabilities such as homeowners insurance, auto insurance, recreational vehicle insurance, and more.

For many people, their home is one of the single largest purchases made in their lifetime, and they would be financially devastated if this were destroyed or unjustly taken from some unfortunate event. This thought also applies to you, a business owner, and protecting your business assets. Whether it is a warehouse, manufacturing plant, office building, rental property, or anything in between, you want protection at the property level. Many are already familiar with property-casualty insurance in the form of homeowners insurance, which generally covers the main dwelling, other structures, personal property, personal liability, medical payments associated with the structure, and the land on which it resides. Make sure to have an annual review with your P&C agent to decide and verify the protection you want.

Umbrella Policy

> **Umbrella policy insurance:** insurance that can protect you from various types of liability claims.

High net worth clients may consider obtaining additional coverage. The easiest coverage to start with is an **umbrella policy**, which you can commence through your property and casualty agent. Everyone should have an umbrella policy. The umbrella policy gives you additional protection above and beyond your regular homeowners policy, automobile policy, and property-casualty policies. These policies usually have to have the maximum liability coverage available before the insurance company will issue an umbrella policy.

The objective with umbrella insurance is to cover your total livelihood (both personal and business wealth) above and beyond the active policies on your assets. You may not need an umbrella policy equal to the whole of your wealth, but the rule of thumb is for the policy to cover enough to deter any liabilities from going after your entire net worth. The cost of these policies is not expensive and can be in the range of $300-$500 annually per $1 million worth of coverage. Talking with your insurance agent and your wealth advisor will help determine your coverage needs.

> Mike, a promising manufacturing business owner, has a net worth in the ballpark of $30 million. In the process of building his dream estate, an uninsured handyman was injured due to an unforeseen hazard. Unfortunately, this event has made Mike liable to incur medical expenses and additional costs for pain and suffering caused. Mike's homeowners insurance has a maximum payment of $500,000, which is not enough for these expenses. Fortunately, before this event, he met with his insurance agent about an umbrella policy. He decided to purchase a $10 million policy with a premium of $2,500 annually. Having this umbrella policy allowed Mike to get through the litigation and expenses without losing his net worth.

Specialty Insurances

There are additional specialized insurances business owners can utilize to protect their assets in exceptional instances not covered in common insurance policies. These policies include captive insurance, long-term care, and board member insurance.

Long-term care policies (LTC) help cover the costs of care and treatment when someone has a chronic illness or disability, mainly in the later stages of their life. This coverage does not directly cover hard assets; it is more of an investment in the event that you or your spouse need long-term care. The investment enables you to draw from insurance coverage instead of using your assets to pay for the expenses. The new generation of LTC coverage should be reviewed to make an informed decision on whether this coverage will help your asset protection strategy.

Directors and officers insurance works similarly to professional liability insurance but focuses instead on board members. This insurance coverage can pay for lawsuits related to decisions made by you and other board members. Coverages can include failures to meet regulatory standards, perform official duties, and accusations of mismanaged funds.

INVESTMENT VEHICLES FOR ASSET PRESERVATION

Tax-efficient accounts such as 401(k)s, IRAs, and Roth IRAs are generally protected from lawsuits and creditors in the interest of justice. These accounts are used mostly in the income tax and retirement savings capacity, but knowing they have a level of protection helps you utilize them to the fullest benefit. Even if income tax savings are not a priority for you, the asset preservation aspect should be since many of these investment vehicles can invest in the same investments as non-retirement accounts.

PRENUPTIAL AGREEMENTS

In addition to using trusts to protect your assets, you should also utilize **prenuptial agreements** with your significant other before getting married. No one getting married expects to get divorced. However, nearly 50% of marriages end in divorce. When a family business and family assets are involved, a prenuptial agreement *should* be implemented. Prenuptial agreements can be an awkward subject to bring up with your future spouse, but it is vitally important that you utilize this asset protection document. Rules and laws vary from state to state. Meet with your estate attorney long before any decisions to marry or before moving to another life stage.

For successful first-generation business owners, your wealth may have been created during your marriage, meaning you did not have a need for a prenuptial agreement. When your heirs are coming of age to get married, discuss prenuptial agreements with them. The future of your business and legacy may depend on it. Many times younger couples will resist this conversation. This is understandable at this stage of their life. However, you likely know couples who got divorced and had financial battles. To compromise with a soon-to-be spouse, simply ensure that the agreement states that any assets you inherited outright will not be split with them in the event of divorce but will be passed on to them in your will, in the event of your death.

Rules and laws vary from state to state. Meet with your estate attorney long before any decisions to marry or you move to another state.

Objective: to protect assets in the event of a divorce.

Pros: maintain separate property and the future of the business or family legacy.

Cons: Possibly uncomfortable conversations.

Professionals: attorney, wealth advisor.

BUSINESS ENTITIES

Business entities may be the single most effective way to limit your personal assets' exposure from business-related liability and lawsuits. People often believe that only their business can be put into an entity such as an LLC. However, the LLC vehicle can also protect other assets such as vacation homes, boats, and airplanes.

Review all of your assets with your estate attorney and property-casualty agent.

Even if you utilize the LLC strategy, you still want liability protection from the LLC's creditors and legal liabilities. Protect all your assets by speaking with the relevant financial professionals.

Objective: protect personal assets from business losses and liabilities.

Pros: protects assets in the event your business is liable for a claim.

Cons: initial formation fees and renewals when setting up an LLC.

Professionals: attorney, property-casualty agent.

TRUSTS

A trust is a form of ownership. The trust creator (grantor) establishes terms of the trust (distribution of income or principal), names the beneficiaries, and chooses the trustee. A trustee is named to oversee the trust and abide by the trust terms. There are two different types of **trusts**: revocable and irrevocable. "**Revocable**" means you can change the terms of the trust, while "**irrevocable**" means that, once the trust is established, the terms are permanent. Once the grantor dies, the revocable trust becomes irrevocable. Irrevocable trusts cannot be modified or amended once they are created. After transferring assets into the trust, the grantor loses all of their rights to the assets.

Using irrevocable trusts, you can control how assets are delivered to your children or grandchildren by the terms you establish in the beginning. Trusts may provide asset protection from liabilities, divorce, and frivolous lawsuits.

In the asset protection side, trusts can be created to protect trust assets from creditors and other various liabilities. Trusts play a major role in estate planning, but you should be aware that these

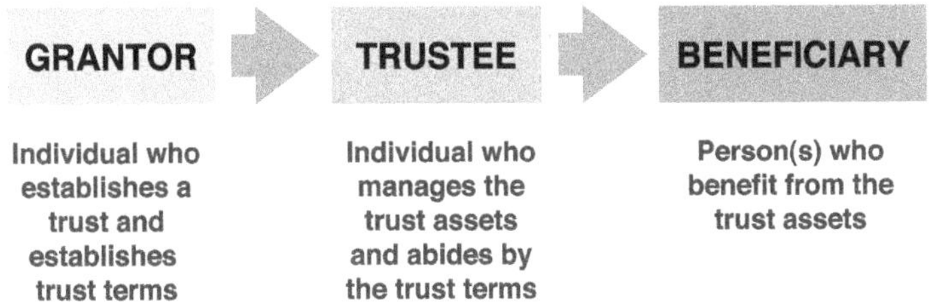

can be used in the asset protection part as well. Consult with an estate attorney on trusts and if any can meet the asset protections you want and deserve.[3]

> **Revocable trust:** a type of trust, which can be changed during a grantor's lifetime, which provides the grantor with flexibility during their life.

> **Irrevocable trust:** a type of trust that cannot be modified or amended. After transferring assets into the trust, the grantor legally loses all of their rights to the assets.

BUY-SELL AGREEMENT

A buy-sell agreement usually states how to transfer a business owner's shares to the surviving owner if one of them dies, becomes disabled, or leaves the company. There are other instances in which shares can be transferred using a buy-sell agreement, but here, only the scenario in which an owner dies will be discussed.

---

3 This information is not intended to be a substitute for individualized legal advice. Please consult your legal advisor regarding your specific situation.

Buy-sell agreement: a contract that states how one partner's share of a business will be distributed if the partner dies, becomes disabled, or leaves the company.

If either you or your business partner dies, the remaining business owner buys out the deceased business owner's estate. This strategy is a good way to protect your business's value so that your surviving spouse or heirs do not have to worry about the future of the company.

Recall the stepped-up basis from Chapter 2. When a business owner dies, their tax basis in the business gets stepped up to the present value. Usually, the buy-sell agreement utilizes life insurance on the owners, and with the proper legal documents, the life insurance proceeds will be income tax-free. The business will use the insurance proceeds to buy the business ownership from the surviving spouse or heir. Because of the stepped-up basis, the surviving spouse or heir will not owe any income tax on the asset.

The buy-sell agreement protects the deceased owner's family at a fair price for the business while the surviving owner will not have to have the deceased owner's family as a business partner.

In summary, there are three benefits with the protection of a buy-sell agreement:

- Protect business asset value.
- Stepped-up basis can eliminate income taxes.
- Less complicated transfer of ownership to remaining business owners.

Objective: to transfer a deceased owner's business assets to surviving owners.
Pros: protects the deceased owner's family at a fair price.
Cons: cost for establishing and insurance premiums.
Professionals: wealth advisor, attorney, business valuation specialist, CPA.

PROTECT YOUR ASSETS

By utilizing the above strategies, including establishing a limited liability company or getting insurance policies, you may be able to effectively protect your assets from lawsuits, creditors, and even divorce. It is best to coordinate among specialized experts to maximize the benefit of each of these asset protection strategies.

Now it is time to educate your heirs on all of your legacy's financial strategies.

ACTION STEPS

What are some of the assets you feel most motivated to protect?

____

Which asset protection strategies would help accomplish your personal objectives?

____

Weigh the pros and cons of each strategy. Which pros are the most appealing to you?

____

Which cons are the least appealing?

____

If you have questions or need more information, reach out to Bill Hrapmann Wealth Advisor, Inc by emailing info@billhrapmann.com.

CHAPTER 5

EDUCATING YOUR HEIRS

Oftentimes, when wealth gets to the next generation, heirs may not know the original story of the wealth or the effort of the accumulation, so they may not behave responsibly with the assets they inherit. When heirs and the next generation are properly educated about the effort, accumulation, and finances, however, they may have a much better opportunity for financial success. Without taking the time to educate your heirs, your future business and wealth may not exist in the future. Heirs could spend above their income means and frivolously waste their inheritance, put financial strain on the business, or lose your hard-earned wealth in a divorce.

For those who do successfully transfer wealth to future generations, what are their strategies? What are they doing differently from those who do not end up getting their wealth to their third generation and beyond?

Educating their heirs is one of the attributes of multi-generational wealth. They are teaching their heirs to live within their means. They teach financial responsibility. By educating your heirs about the origin of your wealth and your financial strategies, you teach them to respect the value of your assets, so they will (hopefully) preserve rather than spend them.

CHAPTER 5

HOW TO EDUCATE YOUR HEIRS

TELLING THE ORIGIN STORY OF YOUR BUSINESS OR WEALTH

Start by telling the history of the business. Most businesses started with a sacrifice or struggle. If you started the business yourself, begin your story from the time you first decided to start your business. What was your inspiration? Your objectives? Your struggles? How many employees at the business's conception? How much did you grow? What did you have to sacrifice? If you took the business over from your parents, tell their story and your personal journey to taking on the role you have today.

Call for a family meeting to explain all that is going on in your company and your personal assets, maybe not all at once but gradually. If you are married, your spouse should be at the meeting. When your children are mature, you want all of your children at the meeting. This is not about age but maturity. Sometimes adults in their thirties are not mature enough to be involved in a business. However, others are mature even as teenagers, eager and excited to be in the business. You have to have the awareness to decide when the right time is to get your heirs involved in learning about your business and finances.

Ideally, members of your Optimal Financial Team will be present. At the beginning, it may be too early to reveal financial assets. That is okay; you may instead discuss your finances in general terms. You may review your investment allocations as percentages, so you do not have to disclose specific values.

Consider keeping the business conversations and your family conversations separate. Hold business meetings to address and take care of the business decisions. You want a designated time to speak about these topics, so they do not spill over to Thanksgiving dinner. If any disagreements arise, they may be contained in the structure

Asset Allocation Chart

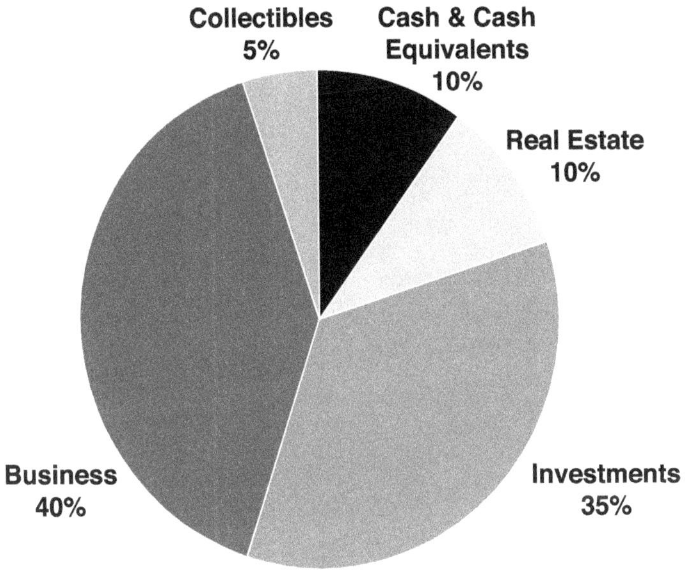

of the family business meeting. When the family business meeting is over, go back to remembering that, at the end of the day, you are family. This business is a whole different entity.

Dividing assets between investment (or business) assets and personal assets can educate your heirs on how to maintain or grow wealth. While investment assets are there to grow and eventually provide you with income, personal assets cost you money to maintain. For example, a house costs you upkeep expenses and real estate taxes, whereas investments/business assets provide income or growth. Clearly outlining your personal assets (high expense potential) and your business assets (high growth potential) can teach how to live within your means. Whether you are making $1,000,000 or $10 million, there is always a limit on spending.

Personal vs. Investment Assets Comparison

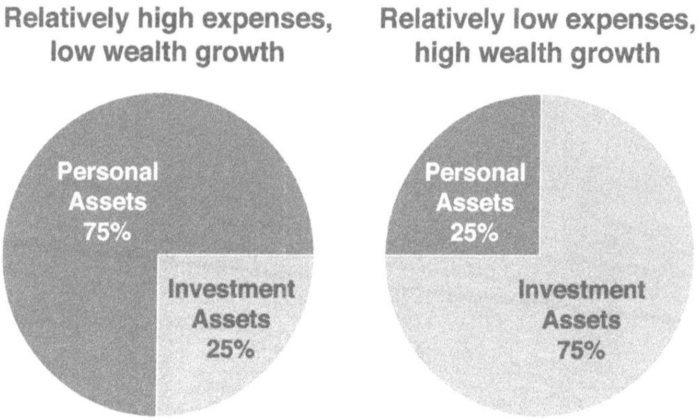

Ideally, as people grow their wealth, investment assets should become a larger percentage, while personal assets should decrease to a smaller percentage of the pie chart.

Bill Hrapmann Wealth Advisor: Financial Miscommunication Leads to Disaster

A new client, who was also recently widowed, Sarah, came to me panicked one day, saying, "What should I do with the business? Do I have enough money?"

It was difficult at first to advise her on anything because we were not familiar with her family's business and personal finances—and neither was anyone else in her family.

Not knowing these vital elements slowed down the whole financial process for my team because we were trying as much as possible to get Sarah up to speed on her family's finances (which took two to three years), as our goal for her was to make prudent financial decisions. Plenty of effort and expertise came from her CPA, tax attorney, and business executives to help with this transition. Transitions can be complicated...are you ready?

The next two sections, "Keeping Business in the Family" and "Keeping Wealth in the Family," will give you more insight into the successful 30% of businesses whose wealth continues to future generations.[4]

KEEPING BUSINESS IN THE FAMILY

In this section, you will learn how to:

- Evaluate who will run your business
- Educate non-participating shareholders
- Protect your shares

DECISION MAKER FOR THE FAMILY AND BUSINESS

If both you and your spouse pass, which of your heirs will be running the business after you are gone? Have they been trained for the role? Who will take on other roles? What is their experience? Are they competent? Do outside factors influence them? Is there more than one child in the business? Will there be shareholders who are not in the business? How will salaries and profits be distributed?

4 Roy Williams and Vic Preisser, *Preparing Your Heirs: Five Steps to a Successful Transition of a Family* (Oregon: Robert Reed Publishers, 2010).

Maybe your spouse is not as involved as you are in the finances, so who will help if something happens to you? Is that person knowledgeable of the objectives that you want to achieve? Are they knowledgeable about your investments? Are they knowledgeable about the assets for different investments that provide additional benefits?

Usually, you have appointed someone to be next in line to run the business. You may be tempted to select your eldest son, but first, consider his skills. Sophisticated companies have a system—job responsibilities, training processes, candidates, and interviews that they take into account before appointing the ongoing decision-maker for the business. Converse openly about your business and have regular family company meetings, as mentioned above.

Suppose you do appoint your eldest son, or another of your offspring, as the ongoing income producer for your family and business. In that case, explain that they should separate their business role and salary from their ownership income (which may fluctuate). What percentage of profits are you paying shareholders? Will there be phantom income? What if there are no profits? You have to define profits (after depreciation, taxes, etc.). Inform your heirs about what they should expect in terms of salary and profits.

At the end of the day, your decision is about trust. Make sure you can trust the person you are selecting. Additionally, as this is not an easy task for the selected person, preparation and training may be beneficial for success in this role.

EDUCATING NON-PARTICIPATING SHAREHOLDERS

In a family business, sometimes family members may not want to be involved with the day-to-day duties and decisions but still want to reap the benefits. In that case, communicating with the non-participating shareholders and keeping them informed about the activities taking place in the business is helpful now and in the future. What income or profits do they expect? Taxes?

Non-participating shareholders of the company are not considered participants in the decision-making process. However, explain that they are still subject to taxation of their share of profits from the business, even if they did not receive them. Remember phantom income.

> Prevent the following scenario that happened to a family business when they reinvested the profits into their business for expansion. At the end of the year, the shareholders received their tax reporting statement, and the non-participating shareholders were surprised they owed hundreds of thousands of dollars in income taxes individually on phantom income. They had to make loans to pay the tax. Ongoing communication can prevent this surprise.

PROTECT YOUR SHARES OF THE BUSINESS

If you want to ensure that your business or wealth gets to future generations beyond your children, you may want to utilize a trust to protect your shares. Within the terms of a trust, your assets may remain protected from any decisions your heirs make. If you are *not* confident that the next generation has a prenuptial or that your wealth will go to the grandchildren, then you can protect your shares by utilizing a trust. Review with your estate attorney.

KEEPING WEALTH IN THE FAMILY

Maybe you are considering selling your business or you inherited significant wealth. In that case, how many generations into the future will this wealth last? Read on to learn about sustaining and even growing your wealth (via your personal assets) over future generations.

In this section, you will learn how to:

- Educate your heirs on your investments.
- Utilize trusts for your objectives.
- Protect your assets by encouraging your children to use prenuptial agreements.
- Keep family heirlooms, if desired.

INVESTMENTS—THE *Why* AND THE *How*

After so many years of hard work, you may have grown investments, stocks, and mutual funds. You have these investments as an inflation hedge for yourself and an accumulation for the next generation, so you may be trying to protect and further grow these assets. You may not need these assets yourself, but you want them to grow for the next generations. Many people become very conservative in their later years. What if you and your spouse do not need the assets or income and you live to 100 years old? That is fifteen more years of potential growth on these investments than the regular life expectancy of living into your mid-eighties. Even though at any time, these investments could go down in value 20% or more, they are for the long-term, so your heirs should know your long-term objectives for all of your assets for them to make prudent decisions.

By educating your heirs on the investments you made, you empower them to make smart decisions about your investments in your portfolio—in the event of your lack of ability or health decline, perhaps, which happens often. You want your children to know what your wishes are, informing them of why you have certain investments in the first place.

Sometimes, the opposite will happen: future generations who did not create the wealth may be overly cautious in protecting it. This caution manifests in highly conservative investments to avoid fluctuating values (they may feel as though they are losing the wealth) but results ultimately in losing purchasing power to inflation.

At BHWA, we call this "getting poor slowly."

However, when future generations learn about investment allocation, investment profiles, and short-term versus long-term investing, they may invest more prudently and preserve your family's and your wealth for generations to come.

UTILIZING A TRUST

A trust is a form of ownership of assets. The grantor or the person who creates the trust may set the terms for the trust. The terms may be how to invest these assets and make distributions and who to name as the beneficiaries.

You decide whether you want a typical entitlement structured trust, an incentive structured trust, or somewhere in-between. An **entitlement-structured trust** is simply determining which heir will receive income or assets, in full or in part, at a certain age or ages with no other requirements. In an incentive structured trust, your heirs will be required to complete certain accomplishments before they can receive any income or assets. For example, if you decided to incentivize education, you can structure the trust to only pay if the beneficiary pursued a degree and maintained a certain grade point average. Entitlement and incentive structured trusts are not legal descriptions. The terms you create in the trust determine whether it is an entitlement- or incentive-structured trust, or somewhere in-between.

To recap, there are two different types of trusts:

- **Revocable trusts:** you may change the terms of the trust or even close the trust

- **Irrevocable trusts:** the terms of the trust cannot be changed once created

Revocable trusts keep assets separate. You may choose for this revocable trust to become irrevocable upon your death. But while you are alive you may make changes to the trust terms as well as move assets in or out of the trust.

Irrevocable trusts are used when you have made absolute decisions about the assets in a trust and how you want the beneficiaries to receive the assets. If this is an entitlement trust, you would simply put how much income or assets each beneficiary should receive at predetermined times. For example, you may have the principle distributed 25% at age thirty, 50% at age thirty-five, and the remaining 100% at age forty.

You could put a trust in your will, which is categorized as a **testamentary trust**. It may be changed anytime until you die or become incoherent. A trust may be used to control the amount of assets, income, or principle that flows to your beneficiaries. You may also control where the assets in the trust go after the beneficiary dies, though there are limits for how many generations the assets can stay in trust. Your estate attorney is the person to rely on.

> For a full review on trusts, see Chapter 3 in sections "Gifting," "Residence Trust," "Intentionally Defective Grantor Trust," "Charitable Trusts," and "Irrevocable Life Insurance Trust" and Chapter 4 in section "Trusts."

PRENUPTIAL AGREEMENTS

Talk to your children about utilizing a prenuptial agreement.

Your child may give you some pushback. They are likely to tell you that they will not get divorced, so they do not need one, but remember, 50% of marriages end in divorce. No one expects to get divorced, but it often happens, and your heir needs to protect their and the family's assets in the event of a split.

Discussing prenuptial agreements with your children when they are young adults twenty to twenty-two years old, or earlier if they are in a serious relationship, really helps them understand the subject of completing a prenuptial agreement. Be prepared; this may not be not a pleasant conversation. Actually a prenuptial agreement can make the intentions very clear and add to a lasting marriage. In the inheritant's will or revocable trust, it can clearly state that there are separate assets that will go to their spouse, eliminating any uncertainties of their intentions.

If a child does not want to implement a prenuptial agreement, then you still have some control over the assets distributed to them with an irrevocable trust. The assets will be distributed according to your wishes, set up in the terms of the trust.

For a reminder of the definition of "prenuptial agreements," see Chapter 4, section "Prenuptial Agreements."

ROTH IRA

In Chapter 2, you read about strategies to mitigate income taxes, which included Roth IRAs, but another way to take advantage of a Roth IRA and teach the next generation at the same time is to have your child set up a Roth IRA once they begin earning income.

This may be a good exercise in learning about income taxes, investing, and saving. As a business owner, you may have children, or nieces and nephews, and they may work at the business, for which you pay them a salary. The salary is deductible to the business. It is taxable to the children, who may have a much lower tax bracket. In this case, the children could contribute after-tax income to a Roth IRA. In 2022, the maximum contribution is $6,000. It may be seen as a small amount of investment, but that investment and future annual contributions can build up substantially over their lifetime.

When they reach retirement age, they may have a tax-free lump of cash. With this strategy, your children will learn about earning money, how to save, and about taxes and investing.

For a full review on Roth IRAs, see Chapter 2, section "Roth IRA."

COLLECTIBLES, SPECIAL ASSETS, AND FAMILY HEIRLOOMS

Some wealthy people get into the hobby of collecting. These collectibles could have substantial worth and increase in value over time. These collectibles could be automobiles, art, coins, and so on. A discussion should occur to inform your heirs of how to continue the collection or liquidate the collection to maximize any financial benefits.

Educate your heirs on the importance of heirlooms, if you have any. It may have significant importance to you and your family's heritage. If that is the case, decide what will happen to the item in the event of your passing. For some items, you may utilize various charitable trusts or even donate to charities that would value these collectibles. For instance, they could go to a museum.

Bill Hrapmann Wealth Advisor: A Special Assets Experience

For special items, such as collections of art or antiques, there is little to no day-to-day expense (other than, possibly, insurance). Heirs may take their time selling those items, if they do indeed want to sell them. For some collections, the value may only be in the eye of the collector. Do not expect the next generations to have the same care and desire to maintain them that you do.

A BHWA client, Patrick, had nearly a hundred mantle clocks—they were beautiful and meant a lot to him and his wife, Johann, who had passed away. He could remember where each one came from. Unfortunately, none of his children wanted those mantle clocks. Patrick wanted to know, "What is going to happen to them? How can my heirs sell them? Should I sell some now or put the burden on my children to sell in the future?"

There is no right answer. It is just a matter of how important it is to you that the collectibles be taken care of, and how.

For a full review on asset protection, see Chapter 4.

CREATE YOUR OPTIMAL FINANCIAL TEAM

Now that you know how to educate and prepare your heirs, you can rest assured that future generations know to take care of your wealth. Now, make plans to discuss your personal and business objectives with financial and specialized experts to protect your wealth and ensure the continued success of your legacy.

In the next chapter, you will learn about the roles that will make up your Optimal Financial Team, though you are already familiar with some of them: your CPA, tax attorney, and wealth advisor are all part of the team.

ACTION STEPS

What do you need to do to set up your first family business meeting?

____

What aspects of your finances and business are important enough to discuss with your heirs?

____

If you have questions or need more information, reach out to Bill Hrapmann Wealth Advisor, Inc by emailing info@billhrapmann.com.

CHAPTER 6

THE WEALTH MANAGEMENT PROCESS AND CREATING AN OPTIMAL FINANCIAL TEAM

This is an unfortunate truth, but oftentimes, wealthy business owners waste a lifetime of effort by not properly preparing and planning for the future. They work hard to go from short sleeves to shirt sleeves, but by the third generation, their family is back to short sleeves again.

You may prevent this horrific imagined future by implementing the wealth management process discussed in this chapter.

WEALTH MANAGEMENT

Wealth management, discussed in broad terms in Chapter 1 and expanded upon in each subsequent chapter, can be a vague concept because it may mean something different to each individual. For this book, define wealth management using this formula, as defined in *The Elite Wealth Manager*[5]:

5 Russ Alan Prince, *The Elite Wealth Manager* (CEG Worldwide, LLC, 2020).

CHAPTER 6

WEALTH MANAGEMENT	=	INVESTMENT CONSULTING	+	ADVANCED PLANNING	+	PROFESSIONAL RELATIONSHIPS

In the next few pages, you will read about each of the three components that equal wealth management.

INVESTMENT CONSULTING

The investment industry has confusing titles for licensed people who implement your investments: investment advisors, financial advisors, financial planners, financial consultants, etc. A professional's investment consulting will also be more tailored to insurance if they have an insurance background; if they have an investment background, their advice will likely lean more toward investments.

To grow to the elite level of wealth advisor, a financial professional must hone experience, knowledge, and independence. As with many professions, education and licenses are just the basics. There is no replacement for professional experience. Would you want your heart surgeon to be fresh out of their residency? Knowledge. Seek out an advisor with advanced certifications such as Certified Financial Planner (CFP®). This denotes dedication to the profession and initial and ongoing education, which keeps the advisor up to date. "Independence" means the wealth advisor does not work exclusively for one corporation that may pressure them to use its products or services. As an independent, your wealth advisor will work for you. You and your family deserve an experienced, knowledgeable, and independent advisor.

We have worked with many business owners who approach us looking for a second opinion/stress test. This in-depth review will help determine whether your current investment strategies are in line with both your personal and business objectives. This second opinion/stress test will either reinforce your current path or pro-

Assessment/Stress Test

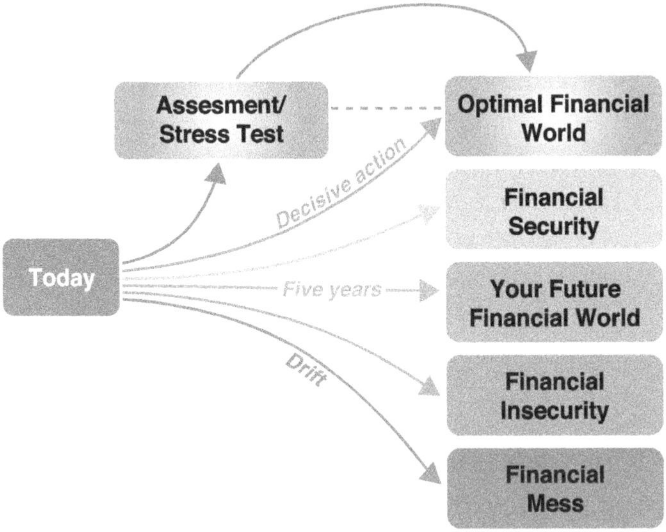

vide suggestions to fill in any gaps to pursue achieving your objectives. Stress testing can help you avoid potentially destructive situations and ensure you benefit from possible opportunities. The Assessment/Stress Test puts you on the fast track to your Optimal Financial World.

ADVANCED PLANNING

Only 6% of advisors in financial services provide this crucial part of wealth management, advanced planning.[6] Advanced planning is the

---

6 Russ Alan Price and John J. Bowen, Jr., *Your Optimal Financial World* (CEG Worldwide, LLC).

coordination of strategies and specialized professionals that pursue your important financial objectives.

We at Bill Hrapmann Wealth Advisor, Inc. emphasize the advanced planning portion of the wealth management process in coordination with your Optimal Financial Team.

The four parts of advanced planning are wealth enhancement, wealth transfer, wealth protection, and charitable giving.

- *Wealth enhancement:* Wealth enhancement mitigates taxes and improves cash flow. Your wealth manager will discuss strategies for this type of enhancement with your CPA, tax attorney, and other necessary professionals to make sure all financial and legal issues are explored.
- *Wealth transfer:* Wealth transfer is the organized transfer of your business and assets to the subsequent owners. Typically, your assets will go to your heirs, people you care about, or charities. Your business may be sold to a third party or passed on to your heirs. Whichever you choose, there are strategies to complete the business transfer to manage and optimize your objectives. The professionals needed are a CPA, a tax attorney, an investment banker, and a business valuation specialist.
- *Wealth protection:* Wealth protection is shielding your wealth from being unjustly taken due to lawsuits, catastrophic events, divorce, or estate taxes. Several strategies exist to protect you: organizing your company as a Corporation or an LLC; utilizing trusts; and insuring against various risks.
- *Charitable gifting:* There are various forms of charitable gifting, from an annual contribution to a family legacy. You may have an interest in providing gifts while you are living, taking advantage of income tax deductions, or you may want to gift after your death and lower your estate taxes. Maybe you want income now and the remainder to go to a charity. Or vice

versa: you want income to go to charity and the principle to go to your heirs.

Since tax laws change, review these strategies with a wealth advisor and your Optimal Financial Team before implementation.

PROFESSIONAL RELATIONSHIPS

The final part of wealth management relates to your professional relationships with a wealth advisor, CPA, tax attorney, or other needed financial specialists. Advanced planning includes continued communication with all of these professionals to move your specific situation forward in the most advantageous way to pursue your objectives.

Specifically, the wealth advisor plays the crucial role of optimizing your wealth management and implementing the wealth management process. The most effective wealth advisors have an advanced business degree and an industry certification, such as Certified Financial Planner, CFP®. They are independent and have ten to fifteen years of experience in the customer-facing financial industry, which is two-plus economic business cycles.

With today's video conferencing, you are not limited to local wealth management. Your wealth advisor may be in a different geographical location than you or your business and still allow you to reap the same benefits and results as if you were meeting in person.

THE PROCESS OF WEALTH MANAGEMENT

Wealth management process: a process of managing wealth that involves financial consultations, planning, and relationship building.

Now you can move on to the process of wealth management. The **wealth management** process can be defined as an organized process to properly develop and execute wealth management (investment consulting + advanced planning + professional relationships). As a business owner, the most efficient elements of your business follow a process instead of a haphazard approach. With your wealth, it should be the same. Over the years, you may have tried to apply haphazard instead of specific financial strategies. Still, perhaps you have never had the benefit of using a systematic process designed specifically for you that coordinates each of your objectives. This is what the wealth management process achieves, and the process for business owners can include unique strategies only available to you as a business owner.

There are five steps involved in the wealth management process:

1. Discovery
2. A review of assets, and evaluation
3. Review meeting
4. Advanced planning
5. Implementation and monitoring

1. DISCOVERY

Discovery is a comprehensive assessment that allows you to review your and your spouse's financial objectives with a wealth advisor. Your wealth advisor will ask you and your spouse a strategic set of questions that identify the importance of these six areas of your life:

- Your personal and financial objectives
- Family and other meaningful relationships
- Business vs. personal assets
- Your professional advisors

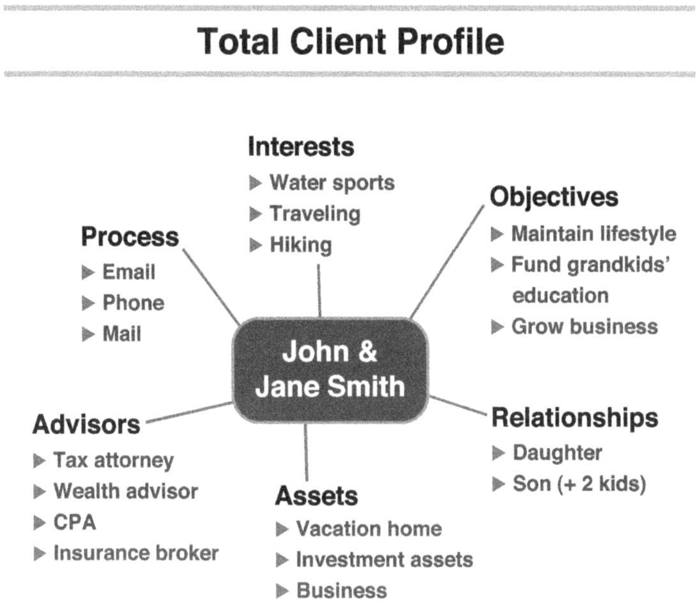

- Communication processes
- Personal interests and hobbies

Your answers will provide a clear understanding of where you are currently with your finances, family, and business. Those answers create your personal profile, which you may share with your other professional advisors to ensure all are working toward your objectives using strategies that pursue the important objectives for you and your family.

2. REVIEW OF ASSETS, AND EVALUATION

Here, your wealth advisor does an in-depth review of your current assets, with an evaluation of if or how these assets will meet your objectives in the most efficient way. The evaluation usually takes about two weeks to complete. When finished, it creates a picture of where you are now, so you and your wealth advisor may determine whether your current assets and strategies will get you where you want to go. Your wealth advisor addresses any gaps that arise, and if necessary, at this time, they may consult with your CPA, tax attorney, or other necessary professionals. This collaboration marks the beginning of your Optimal Financial Team.

Oftentimes, a business owner may have non-business investments that do not match their individual investor profile. They could be overly conservative, minimizing their future wealth, or overly aggressive, bringing more uncertainty into their assets than is in line with your investor profile. Aligning your investment choices with your specific objectives is vital to meet your objectives.

3. REVIEW MEETING

You and your wealth advisor will meet (physically or via video conference) to review your personal profile and your current assets. It is essential to provide detailed information and maintain clear communication throughout this process. The wealth advisor's focus will be on making sure that your current assets meet your objectives cost-effectively. The review meeting will also include discussions on estate strategies and the future of your business.

4. ADVANCED PLANNING

In this advanced planning step, your wealth advisor will review your personal profile with your CPA, tax attorney, and other necessary advisors, such as your property and casualty agent or investment banker. You may want to participate in this step. For instance, there may be estate strategies to save estate taxes by gifting assets, and your Optimal Financial Team may require your input.

This review with all of your professionals ensures each professional's awareness of your objectives. Together, your professionals use their expertise to better align your finances with your objectives or implement any relevant strategies. This is where "advice" turns into an efficient, powerful path forward for you, your family, and your business.

5. IMPLEMENTATION AND MONITORING

The wealth management process is not static; it is ongoing. Monitoring your circumstances and communication with your CPA, tax attorney, and wealth advisor will be necessary to keep your plan current and on its ideal path. Depending on the complexity of your situation, these professionals will determine the time frame for ongoing reviews and meetings during this step.

OPTIMAL FINANCIAL TEAM

Now that you have read through the thoughts and processes that go into managing your wealth and legacy, you may realize the needed depth and knowledge to properly align your strategies with your objectives. As mentioned in Chapter 1, utilizing an Optimal Financial Team can help tremendously in reducing your efforts, time, and possible missed items in regards to your wealth management.

This open communicating mindset among you and your professionals brings everyone to the same understanding and can further help you achieve your financial and personal objectives. Take advantage of this network of expertise, experience, and knowledge that could only be acquired from professionals in each particular financial or legal area. Knowing your professionals are getting the right information to best serve your objectives will benefit all parties involved, especially you, the business owner.

WHO SHOULD BE ON YOUR OPTIMAL FINANCIAL TEAM?

Your team may consist of:

- Certified Public Accountant (CPA)
- Tax attorney
- Property-casualty insurance agent
- Corporate attorney
- Investment banker
- Wealth advisor

Certified Public Accountant (CPA)

You may want to review your corporate structure with your tax expert to determine whether it is more advantageous to structure your company as a C Corp or an S Corp or even a partnership. Different tax laws apply to each, and your CPA will be able to advise you if restructuring to one or the other could be beneficial to you.

CPAs can help with gifting assets to minimize taxes, utilizing trusts, guiding on adopting buy-sell agreements, and the benefits of retirement plans.

Tax Attorney

A business owner would want to meet with their tax attorney (sometimes called an estate attorney) every three to five years to ensure the value of their estate and mitigate tax expenses from year to year. This is the time to start making estate strategies and minimizing future estate tax.

Tax attorneys help minimize income and estate taxes by guiding individuals through strategies such as utilizing trusts, retirement plans, properly structured wills, prenuptial agreements, and other legal matters.

P&C Insurance Agent

Your P&C insurance agent will review your needs and provide coverage where necessary. It is crucial to have your insurance requirements in order in a worst-case scenario, such as a fire that destroys your factory. The importance of an annual review of your property-casualty coverage cannot be underestimated.

Insurance agents help set up different types of insurance to help you protect your assets. These insurances include umbrella policy, property-casualty insurance, homeowners insurance, and board member insurance.

Corporate Attorney

Your corporate attorney should be engaged three to five years ahead of time if you are planning on selling your business. This ensures all corporate papers are in order. If shares exist, your share certificates and share ledger must be accurate and up-to-date. Any leases that may be active on property, whether to a third party or yourself, should be carefully reassessed to update them to lock in a future income. If you intend to protect the job of any personnel, you may want to implement a deferred compensation package for those employees, which would keep them tied to the business after a sale. These details can place you in an ideal position to sell if you so desire.

Investment Bankers

In the event you want to sell your business, the investment banker has several functions. They make sure your documents are in good order and make suggestions to maximize the value of your business. They assist with comparing similar companies that have been sold and any attributes that led to a higher sale price. Since investment bankers are in constant contact with potential buyers, they constantly communicate with buyers and sellers at the business level. The investment banker might also locate potential buyers.

If your buyer requires financing, you will likely be engaging to some extent with *their* investment banker as they are often the financiers of these transactions. Your corporate attorney will assist you with any terms and draw up the necessary contracts to manage this process.

Wealth Advisor

Your wealth advisor evaluates, coordinates, and manages your financial investments along with assisting in the mediation of your estate and tax objectives with the relevant professional.

Wealth Advisors across the industry all have access, in general, to all the same or similar investments and strategies. All these investments, strategies, and products can be thought of as "table stakes;" every wealth advisor is playing in the same sandbox.

Wealth advisors differentiate themselves in their experience, certifications, and collaborating with other professionals. An elite wealth advisor has extensive experience and collaborates with your other professionals. They should provide personalized strategies to best match your objectives. An elite wealth advisor should serve you and your personalized objectives to decide which investments and strategies will work best. They should look at your total financial picture and assess what is important to you as a business owner. Your wealth advisor should be of elite status within the industry. See Wealth Management Hierarchy below.

What short-term objectives would you want to achieve in this phase of your life? What long-term objectives? How much income do you need to maintain your current lifestyle and still have enough to meet these objectives? What tax strategies might save you thousands in unnecessary tax payouts?

IN SUMMARY

By taking advantage of the Optimal Financial Team and working together as a team of experts, you are taking advantage of each pro-

The Wealth Management Hierarchy

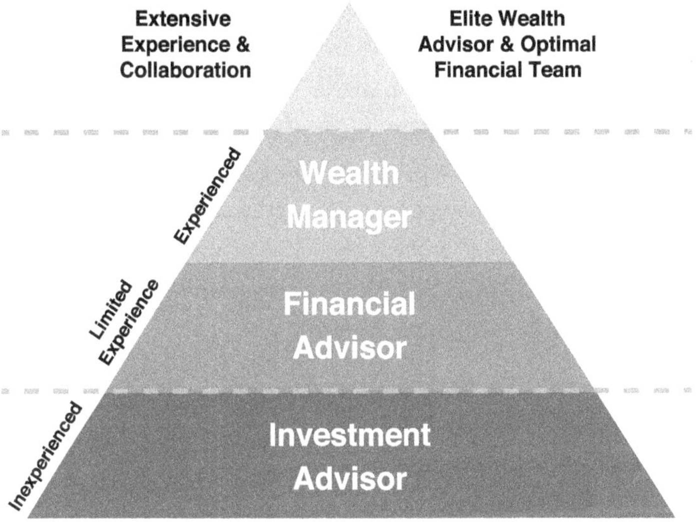

fessional's valuable input. They all have their own specialties that cross over to each other, which may help optimize your finances.

Somebody must be the general manager of the team of experts. Usually, your wealth advisor takes on this role, but you may choose to select your CPA or tax attorney to serve as general manager instead. Who the general manager is does not matter so much, but *somebody* must be proactive in the communication cycle.

Oftentimes, the wealth advisor gathers all of the data to create your personal profile. This information, or other in-depth information, about your objectives could be important to you and achieving your objectives. For instance, typically, one of your professionals may not know that you have three children and five grandchildren.

Every six months, or sooner if there are major changes in your circumstances or tax law changes, have a meeting with your Optimal Financial Team.

Save time and costs by coordinating you and your professionals on your financial team together to discuss how to accomplish your objectives even better. The professionals on your financial team need to be sure they are all on the same page. With no coordinated communication, it would take plenty of time and costs to keep going back and forth with your professionals. But, when there is coordinated communication similar to an Optimal Financial Team, you may jump from a long process to a shorter time frame. Everyone will be more efficient, cutting the time to completion from years to maybe six months to eighteen months.

ACTION STEPS

Think back on your personal financial objectives. Are there any areas in which you think utilizing an Optimal Financial Team would have worked better?

____

Likewise, consider your business objectives. Which professionals can help you accomplish them?

____

If you have questions or need more information, reach out to Bill Hrapmann Wealth Advisor, Inc by emailing info@billhrapmann.com.

CONCLUSION

When considering how to best achieve your objectives, you want sound personalized strategies that will assist you in meeting these. This book has taught you how to successfully apply techniques to save money on income and estate taxes, protect your assets, and educate your heirs.

In **Chapter 1**, you felt the pulse of your business and your overall finances, separating your personal and business assets and considering concepts that can keep your business thriving even in the wake of modern innovations. **Chapter 1** also introduces the Optimal Financial Team and the benefits of utilizing your professional resources to better achieve your personalized financial objectives. In **Chapters 2–5**, you learned specific tax, asset, and heir strategies, and in **Chapter 6**, the Wealth Management Process was introduced along with the major professionals who could help achieve your financial objectives. When these professionals are coordinated into an Optimal Financial Team, the communication and your financial future can be optimized.

TAXES

In **Chapters 2 and 3**, you learned that many business owners take advantage of many tax-saving strategies. Some of these include establishing a captive insurance policy with tax-advantaged features, implementing a specialized retirement plan which may substantially increase the tax-deductible contributions for yourself, and gifting company shares to keep you in control while potentially decreasing estate taxes.

ASSETS

In **Chapter 4**, you learned about asset protection, a strategy that aims to safeguard both your business and personal assets from creditors and lawsuits and uncontrolled spending by future generations. Your Optimal Financial Team can easily manage these various types of asset protection strategies.

HEIRS

In **Chapter 5**, you learned how to secure your assets in the future so that you may enjoy your retirement and how educating heirs on your financial strategies can help ensure they will be taken care of when you pass.

It is essential to take the time to analyze your business objectives and needs. A comprehensive assessment helps you identify areas to improve your wealth management strategy. When was the last time you had a comprehensive assessment of your finances? Was your Optimal Financial Team included in the assessment? This book has helped you identify your financial objectives and provided you with a process to improve your finances even more.

As you read in **Chapter 6**, the wealth management process reviews where you are today, where you want to go, and fills in any gaps to get there. Having an Optimal Financial Team can make this process even better.

What is important to you when it comes to your finances? What are your objectives? You decide!

To better answer those questions, consider all the answers you wrote down in the *Action Steps* sections of each chapter. If you have been reading this book straight through, here are all the questions again for your convenience.

ACTION STEPS

Take a few minutes to gather a generalized list of your personal assets:

____

Do the same for your business assets:

____

What are your top three business objectives?

____

What are your top three personal objectives?

____

Consider which company tax structure would be most beneficial for your business.

____

Which income tax strategies would you be interested in learning more about?

____

What is the estimated value of your taxable estate?

____

Which estate tax strategies do you feel would help meet your objectives?

____

What are some of the assets you feel most motivated to protect?

____

Which asset protection strategies would help accomplish your personal objectives?

____

Weigh the pros and cons of each asset protection strategy (property-casualty insurance, LLCs, buy-sell agreements, trust, prenuptial agreements). Which pros are the most appealing to you?

____

Which cons are the least appealing?

____

What do you need to do to set up your first family business meeting?

____

What aspects of your finances and business are important enough to discuss with your heirs?

____

Think back on your personal financial objectives. Are there any areas in which you think utilizing an Optimal Financial Team would have worked better?

____

Likewise, consider your business objectives. Which professionals can help you accomplish them?

____

From here, your wealth advisor should assess your current financial strategies and investments to perform a stress test. They will ask you questions like:

- What if you died prematurely?
- What if you sold your business, or only half of your business?
- What if your top executives left your company?
- What if technology made your product or services obsolete?
- What will happen to your wealth when you retire?
- Do you have a medical power of attorney?
- Will your family stay united when you are gone?
- Are your wills in line with your objectives?

After getting all this necessary information, your wealth advisor and Optimal Financial Team will suggest strategies to even better position your finances in preparation for all these what-ifs. You and your spouse will decide which strategies to implement.

Expose any holes in your financial health. There is always at least one hole, and when you meet with your Optimal Financial Team once a year, this is your opportunity to spot holes and fill them in. If you are not finding holes, you are not stress testing well enough.

Review your financial strategies every two or three years, or more frequently if your schedule permits. Let your Optimal Financial Team know if anything has changed (for example, tax laws, family changes, business structure changes, etc.). Here are some reasons you may need to sit down with your Optimal Financial Team to change your long-term financial strategies:

- You had more children or more grandchildren
- You got a divorce (knock on wood)
- You sold a percentage of your business
- You sold your business outright
- You brought in a partner
- Your adult child(ren) is (are) now in the business
- You gifted shares of your business

Managing your wealth is an important step in your life. Often, people who own businesses and are wealthy have many skills, but they rarely learn how to optimize their finances. Regardless of the size of your business, you may use sound financial strategies to improve your current and future financial health.

As a business owner, you have additional opportunities to have personalized strategies for your finances, minimize income and estate taxes, accumulate and distribute assets, and take care of heirs. You may start this process by becoming aware of the wealth management strategies for business owners mentioned in this book.

Although this book certainly does not cover all of the available strategies, your Optimal Financial Team can work together to fill in the gaps.

Now that you have come to the end of this book, take action, become even more financially prepared, and work toward achieving your financial objectives. Have your estate pass on to your heirs according to your terms. If you have questions or need more information, reach out to Bill Hrapmann Wealth Advisor, Inc by emailing info@billhrapmann.com.

ABOUT THE AUTHORS

BILL HRAPMANN, CFP®, CRPC®

Bill has been helping business owners pursue their objectives for forty years.

Bill is a third-generation business owner: both of his grandfathers, his father, and his uncles were all business owners. Bill gained valuable insight on running a business from growing up in this environment, including developing a can-do and achievement-oriented approach to helping business owners achieve their important objectives.

Today Bill helps business owners and retirees pursue their financial objectives by developing and managing customized portfolios. His first experience with investing was in the mid-1970s when he was in high school where he started investing his earnings from his lawn care & home maintenance business. In addition to managing client investments, Bill and his son Chad create Optimal Financial Teams for clients, enabling professional collaboration that pursues financial health and mitigates vulnerabilities.

After earning a business degree from Tulane University and an MBA from the University of New Orleans, Bill is an independent wealth advisor and the president of Bill Hrapmann Wealth Advisor, Inc. He holds the Certified Financial Planner™ (CFP®) certification and is a Certified Retirement Planning Consultant (CRPC®).

CHAD HRAPMANN, MBA

Chad is planning to become a fourth-generation business owner.

He provides analytical and technical expertise with his background as a licensed civil engineer. Chad makes wealth management relevant to future generations of business owners.

Chad's interest in financial planning stems from his early experiences in the financial world: his father and coauthor, Bill, taught him at an early age about investing, and Chad would even contribute a portion his earnings to a Roth IRA to learn about investing.

After graduating with a bachelor's degree in Civil Engineering at Louisiana State University, Chad first worked in the oil and gas industry and industrial construction. Through his engineering education and early work experience, Chad developed a different perspective on financial advising and problem-solving, which has served his clients well. On top of his engineering degree, Chad also has a Master's in Business Administration from the University of New Orleans.

Chad is an independent wealth advisor and associate with Bill Hrapmann Wealth Advisor, Inc and is also pursuing a Certified Financial Planner™ (CFP®) certification.

CPSIA information can be obtained
at www.ICGtesting.com
Printed in the USA
JSHW051512201122
33501JS00004B/10/J

9 781544 530727